Choose Life

CHOOSE LIFE

Live the life Christ died for you to have.

Joanna .N. Douglas

True Freedom Books

ISBN: 978-0-9935856-0-9

Please note that it is the author's intention to glorify God in all He does in His three person's of God the Father, Jesus Christ the Son and Holy Spirit and so uses the capitalization of His names and pronouns. The author does not give any glory to satan and so does not use the capitalization his name or pronouns even at the beginning of a sentence, which may differ from the publication edition of the bible given above.

First published in 2016 in Great Britain by True Freedom Books.

If you wish to contact Joanna .N. Douglas or True Freedom Books or for any other information Please visit;

www.joannadouglas.wix.com/truefreedombooks

For Josephine:
The girl who never gave up.

The Lord is the Spirit; Where the Spirit of the Lord is there is FREEDOM.

- 2 Corinthians 3:17

WITH THANKS

First and foremost I want to thank my best friend, my first love, my beautiful Lord Jesus Christ. Amazing, perfect and wonderful in everyway, for without Him I would not have survived, I would not know freedom and so there would be no book to write.

To my Mum and Dad for loving me and caring for me deeply. For being such amazing parents, and for supporting me and caring for me, as they watched their happy content child slip away from them into an angry mess. For bringing me up to know Jesus, and for supporting me on my journey to freedom.

To my sister Becky, who has watched me and supported me in some of the darkest times in my life. Who I have looked up to and aspired to be like, who will always be a woman I admire.

To the church of my childhood who taught me, nurtured me and helped me to move in the ways of the Spirit at a young age. Who brought me up to know God, and who supported me in my faith throughout my teen years.

To my first Bible College for showing me beyond doubt my academic ability. For showing me a love for deeper biblical knowledge could be combined with a real faith. To the staff there who cared for me the best way they knew how.

To my Yorkshire family who gave me a place to heal for a number of months when there seemed nowhere else to turn to. For giving me a home to rest, heal and restore. You gave me a very special place to meet with Jesus and to grow but most importantly to soften my hardened heart. To the women I lived with during my time there, each in their own way inspiring me. Also a deep thank you to the women who cared for me, and supported me while I was there, and demonstrated the true beauty of God's love and compassion.

To my Spiritual home on the Wirral. A community who welcomed me into their home and lives as I journeyed further into healing and freedom.

To St. Mary's my beautiful home church and place of belonging. A church who welcomed me in my utter brokenness and loved me back to life. To all my friends there and especially to my 20s – 30s small group, who are beautiful friends who have become a reminder of how far I've come over the years. Also a special deep gratitude to those at St. Mary's who walked a long and difficult journey alongside me for my healing. A journey that was beyond the possible without Jesus at their side. Those amazing people who never gave up on me or my healing no matter what the cost. Who continued to stand with me believing in a bright and beautiful future that I could not see. Those few at St. Mary's who gave their all to see me, a hurting, broken, angry and torn apart woman restored and whole in Christ.

To the Light Project and my new Chester family for believing in me and inspiring me to serve the Lord, and for equipping me and inspiring me to publish this book. For being the beginning of that bright and beautiful future in Christ that I finally see.

To all those who have supported me on the journey to freedom, and to those who helped me to get this book in print.

And lastly to all the others, the little ones, who's bravery, and persistent declaration that Jesus is Lord, will never be forgotten.

CONTENTS

THE STARTING POINT

You are loved very dearly; you are created by One who loves every part of you. You are a saint, and you are fully secure and chosen by the One who knows you and loves you. He has a plan for your life, and He desires to know you more and more. He is alive and active in the world today. You are made special and just as you were designed to be. You are beautiful, precious, wanted, and dearly loved and valued. You carry great wisdom and purpose. Your dreams and hopes will be fulfilled.

The love of the creator of the entire universe holds you dearly, His love never stops existing. You are meant to be in this world. You have your place and a home and a family in your creator. You were made for a reason and placed where you are for a purpose. God has not forgotten you. You are not abandoned, hated, or rejected. You are loved with such passion that your heart can rest. No matter what you have been through, you can be at peace and at rest in the full assurance that the creator who made you loves you with an everlasting love.

God is the creator of the universe, divine in nature and sovereign in power. He is the King of all things. Full of power and wisdom, His authority is absolute and His compassion great and healing. He exists in three separate persons—God the Father, Jesus the Son, and Holy Spirit, and yet the three together in complete unity are one God. God is omnipresent, meaning He can be everywhere at once. He is outside of time and outside of our geographical understanding of the world. "God is love" (1 John 4:8). God is good, and to be free is to live in His goodness with a great peace and intimacy with Him not bound by shame or anger or bitterness.

I cannot heal you, and this book will not heal you. Your church leader cannot heal you, nor can your church friend or your prayer partner. But the good news is that your loving God can! He can meet you, transform you, and heal you. In Him you can be changed and restored.

I had the privilege of having my 16th birthday in Tanzania in east Africa. My unforgettable time there changed and shaped me forever. A family in my church were missionaries in a rural village there. My youth leader and other members of the church accompanied four of us from the youth group. Although I was keen to sign up and go, I must admit that I did not know what I was in for. My

Mum and Dad were *not* keen for me to go because I was not only young but rather immature for my age. At that point in my life, I was a very confused and hurting person. God had His plan, though, and so in the summer of 2004 I flew off to Tanzania without my parents and saw life in Africa. I did not go on a pre-organized mission with a charity staying in a hotel and doing some project in the village. I stayed in the village and in a way I got to experience life in the village and a little of what it was really like to be a missionary in a poorer country.

I saw God there in a way that really touched me. I had the opportunity to visit a hospital in that east African village and went to visit a few patients there. That was a moment in my life as a teenager that impacted me more than I realised at the time. Two of the patients I met and prayed with in the hospital died while I was still in Tanzania, both died for reasons that in a western hospital they would probably not have died. Somehow that experience changed me. It brought me back to the God I had been falling away from. At that moment in my life I knew that I wanted to give my life entirely to serve the Lord wherever He led me. Yet healing was not instant. It took time and was hard and sometimes seemed impossible.

I make no promises for this book. It cannot heal you

or help you—only God can. I have simply put together a short whistle-stop tour of the last 12 years of my journey of healing from that moment in Tanzania to where I am today. I am just now beginning to know what it is to be free in Jesus and in a place to be able to serve Him. It is my prayer that as I share a tiny bit of my journey and the tools I learnt along the way God will reach you and help you along your way in your journey to healing and freedom.

The roots of our pains and struggles go very deep. The world is a harsh place, and sometimes we face trials so hard for us to bear. The Bible says God will never let us face more than we can bear. I hated that verse—1 Corinthians 10:13—for so long. There have been many times in my life when I have faced more struggles than I felt I could bear. That might be true for you, too. But, hold on, because you will learn, as I did, that Jesus was there in your pain. So often we look at the darkest times in our life and question where He was. You need to know, He was there. He cared then and He cares now. His heart is moved so very deeply by our brokenness. I have come to learn and understand that God was there in my pain, that He was there in my darkness and has wept with me. He has never taken me through more than I can bear because I am alive today. I am not only alive but free! I am living my life for Him, and I am doing the things I love. The reason I could bear what seemed like unbearable trials was that God was there at my side all the while. I am alive and I have been set free from my pains to choose life. The same is true for you too! It is time to begin to choose life.

I am not in any way saying life is perfect now. I face struggles and sometimes I feel like it's one struggle after the other. Anxiety still fills me and sometimes I feel like I am going backwards to who I used to be but I am not. In Jesus I am secure and He walks with me in my trials. He will do the same for you if you let Him.

I pray now in the name of Jesus that as you begin to turn the pages and read this book a true freedom will be released into you. I pray that anything that would seek to stop you from reading this book will be taken from you through Jesus Christ. I pray that you will have clarity of mind, heart, and spirit as you engage with your loving creator through the reading of this book and embarking on your journey towards freedom. I pray that what you need to read and get out of this book will sink into your soul and take root and grow. I pray that anything that is not relevant to you will not be a stumbling block to your engaging with the One who loves you and created you. I pray protection and a filling of God's love and peace in you as you meet with Him on your journey to living the life Christ died for you to have. May he bless you beyond anything you have ever dared to imagine. Amen.

INTRODUCTION

I grew up in a loving Christian home. There was my Mum and Dad, my older sister, and me. From my earliest memory we went to church. I liked church. I had friends there and enjoyed Sunday school. It was a good family Anglican Church in inner city Manchester. When I was a young child life was good and enjoyable. I was a very happy, bright, and confident child. I was always smiling. I loved life. I loved to imagine and dress up and play exciting and complex imaginary games. I met God in a very profound way at a very young age.

Yet my happy content childhood began to slip away from me in primary school. From a young age I was bullied at school and suddenly found that I was not feeling happy and content anymore. Slowly my smiling face began to smile less and less. My confidence in who I was drifted more and more away from me, and I found myself looking in the mirror and hating what I saw. That tiny child I was who knew God in such a profound way stopped knowing how to trust in Him. I stopped caring about myself and soon stopped caring about anything or anyone. Sometimes it felt as though I had stopped living. Inside I felt so empty, but I didn't know how to talk or express how I felt. I didn't even know why I felt that way and for so long I didn't even notice I was feeling that way. I felt dead, ashamed, and lost. I did not want to live this way and did not know why I felt so hurt. I could not explain it. It was because of that my relationship with God suffered over the years. I have never not known God and I have never blamed Him but I stopped turning to Him for help in my struggles.

God's original design for mankind was something very beautiful. God designed us to walk with Him in complete unity and intimate relationship. It was supposed to be that beautiful image of God walking with Adam in the Garden that we read about in Genesis. All was perfect until satan introduced corruption. satan—then called lucifer—was an angel very close to the throne of God. He swelled up with pride, however, and tried to be God, and so God threw him out of Heaven along with the other angels who were corrupted. God did this because nothing that is not of God or aligned with Him and His nature can be in Heaven.

After God created Adam and Eve, satan was so jealous of God's beautiful and intimate relationship with them that he tried to corrupt the relationship between God and mankind. In many ways it appeared as though he had succeeded. satan has succeeded in bringing sin into the world, and he tempts people to live a life outside of what God wants for them. satan is the prince of lies and will convince us of lies to bring death and decay. In this way satan traps us. Through fear, anger, shame, guilt, and condemnation, satan convinces us that we can never live in the beautiful closeness with God that He intended for us. satan wants us to believe we are trapped in the brokenness he wants us to stay in. He does not want us to be close to God and will do anything in his power to stop us from living the beautiful, free, and secure life God intended for us.

satan steals life from us and takes pleasure in our demise and in the destruction of our close relationship with God. Many say that satan does not have power, but he does. satan uses many things to entice us to fall into his trap. The Bible describes satan as a very beautiful being who appears as an angel of light, who deceptively tries to trick us into following his ways (2 Corinthians 11:14). Many of us end up dabbling in his occult ways because he is a master at dressing up dangerous and corrupt things so they look beautiful; he makes addictive behaviours seem like harmless fun. When I refer to satan in this book, I am referring to him as a personable identity, a fallen angel with his own thoughts and feelings of hate and pride.

Yet it is also important to recognise that as a created being satan is *not* omnipresent as God is. This means that neither satan nor his army of corrupted angels called demons or unclean spirits can be in more than one place at a time. When I refer to satan in this book I am referring to his demonic realm and all things that are of him and not of God. Since he cannot personally be in every person's life, his followers or demons affect us more.

The story doesn't end here, though! Rejoice, for God has overcome satan! The beautiful thing is that God is so much bigger than satan. God's power is greater, and He has not left us to satan. God loves us and has sent His Son, Jesus, to die for us—to bring us freedom and a restored intimate relationship with God. Although that freedom can come instantly through divine intervention, in most cases it is a journey, a wonderful journey, one that God walks with us on. However it is a hard journey and one we need to be prepared to choose, but through it we do not have to live in fear, anger, shame, and guilt. We do not have to live feeling broken and dead inside. God in His love and mercy looks at us with such wonder and grace. Through that love, and *because of* that love, He has saved us and given us life. Once you have a love encounter with Jesus, you will never be the same because He will change you for the better as He walks in intimate relationship with you. Jesus restores and redeems us through His death and resurrection. Join with Holy Spirit and allow Him to take you on the wondrous and powerful journey out of death to life. It is a beautiful thing; it is possible to be in relationship with God in a place of peace and freedom. It is a battle and a fight to stand free, but your fight is not against God nor is it against flesh and blood. Your fight is against satan and the powers of this world. (Ephesians 6:12) Rejoice because God will smash the chains that bind us if we will only choose life. He has already given us the tools for life, and now it is time for you to start living the life Christ died for you to have.

Now when I look in the mirror I like what I see. I smile and laugh and dance. I speak in confidence and know that I can rest in full assurance of who I am and who Jesus is. I am filled with the wonder of life and the power of God. I am excited to live a life expectant of the wonderful things Jesus has in store for me. I walk side by side with God, and I am growing and learning to walk with Him intimately. I know what it is to be completely forgiven and redeemed from all my sins. I feel completely overjoyed by the work of God in my life. My life has taken off in wondrous ways I never dared to dream it would.

I am not merely alive but I *love life* and am full of God's love, forgiveness, and overwhelming power. I am currently studying a degree in theology, mission and evangelism and am excited about where my journey with God will lead me in this beautiful world. I have traveled alone yet with great confidence to different countries to see the wonder of God's creation. As I said before not everything in my life is wonderful now or perfect, nor will it ever be till I am in Heaven but I am finding myself more and more on a journey through which I am fast becoming what God means for me to be.

I am no longer just waiting to die with no expectations for my future. I no longer look in the mirror and hate what I see. Fear and shame no longer trap me. I am at peace. Though I struggle and face difficulties in the world, I have the tools to face those struggles side-by-side and shoulder-to-shoulder with my Lord, and I choose to use those tools more and more until they become natural. My faith and my emotions are restored to that tiny little girl I used to be. I am excited about where God is going to take me. Life is for living. God meant for us to enjoy life. Live the life Christ died for you to have. It is a choice. Choose life. Join me as I share with you my story and the tools I learnt along the way. Allow God to meet you and to walk intimately with you.

In some sections of this book I have written some examples of prayers you could pray into each situation. If you have your own prayers or words you want to say feel free to use your own words. The example prayers are just a guide if you don't know what else to say.

CHAPTER ONE

GOD'S LITTLE GIRL

On the 20th January 1994, 120 people met in a church close to Toronto Airport in Canada. What happened in that meeting has been called 'crazy', 'wild', and 'unusual'. It was unprecedented. It was unexpected. It was uncontainable. In the months and years that followed, so many lives all around the world were touched, moved, and transformed by the move of God that began that day in Canada. That move of God is still active today. What has become known as The Toronto Blessing or The Father's Blessing has impacted countless lives. On the 20th January 1994, God's Holy Spirit moved in that church in a way that grew to be a worldwide phenomenon. Through the move that continued on from that day, Holy Spirit has touched the lives of thousands of people, believers and non-believers alike. Many people have met God because of the Toronto Blessing as well as the Charismatic revivals, and John Wilber's power evangelism movement.

We are blessed to be living in the post-Charismatic Revival age. I cannot say when I first considered who Holy Spirit was or when I first thought about what it meant to be living post-revival, but I can say I knew Holy Spirit as a young child. I saw visions and dreamed dreams, I talked in heavenly tongues and understood and interpreted many dreams and visions. I would shake and fall to the floor resting in God from my earliest childhood. Although terms such as being 'baptized in the Spirit' was not something I understood, I did see angels at my side and Jesus was a constant and very real companion.

I first met Holy Spirit in the summer of 1994, at the tender age of 6 years old. My family and I went with a number of people from the Anglican Church we were attending to New Wine Christian summer conference in Shepton Mallet. Like many people at that time, my parents were skeptical of this great move of the Spirit, and I think they were going in part at least to try to prove it wasn't real. During that weeklong camping conference, however, my parents and many others from our church were touched by 'the wave' of the Spirit. Holy Spirit filled that campsite that year, and from what I have come to understand it was almost impossible for anyone to remain skeptical of His great signs and wonders. Though I was a child and knew nothing of the idea of Charismatic revival, I do remember standing in the children's tent one evening—an evening I could never forget, an evening that has changed the course of my life forever.

That was a moment in my history that would later lead to my ultimate survival. As I stood there singing the Jesus songs, I watched as children fell to the floor. I heard some of the leaders crying and singing beautifully in a language I did not know or understand. I watched as children as young as I was fell to the floor laughing, and I saw my leaders who were probably younger than I am now shaking and shining with a bright light. The tent glowed, and as I looked up towards the bright light above, I saw moving above me what I have later come to know as angels. I clenched my fists. I knew it was God and that He was moving safely among us. I don't know how I knew, but I just seemed to know that it was God. I knew *of* God and yet that was the day, the moment, that I came to *know* God, the moment my salvation was sealed and secure. From that moment on in my life I have been a follower and believer of God.

I was not afraid, but I used to clench my fists when I wanted to be near Jesus and pretend I was holding His hands. There I was, just turned 6 years old, tiny and young for my age in wondrous awe as the heavens opened above me. I knew nothing of the difference between God or Holy Spirit. I knew of Jesus and I knew the Bible stories, but I was too young to know of the Trinity. Yet I knew enough to know this was God. With tiny fists clenched, I looked up to the angels above the tent and I asked God for what everyone else seemed to have that day. In that second, great warmth filled my troubled child's mind. I had begun to feel a constant worry in my mind and yet here I felt a peace, a safety, and a warmth I had lost somehow. I felt this warmth and peace spreading from my head to my toes like a current of overwhelming electricity. Then I fell, but not like a trip or a fall but as though I was falling in slow motion to the floor, being blown over by such a powerful yet gentle, invisible force before closing my eyes as if asleep.

A wave of peace filled me. I had never felt anything so safe and so wonderful in my life. It was not what I had expected, though I cannot say I know what I had really expected. As I lay there on the floor of that tent I wasn't really aware of what was going on around me, though I don't think that really matters. Yet I was very acutely aware of what was going on *inside of* me.

A vision began to fill my mind—a vision so vivid I remember it as though it were yesterday. It is still so very real in my mind more than 20 years on. In my vision there was a heart, a human heart, though at that age I don't think I had ever seen an image of a human heart. Yet I knew it was a heart, my heart. A dark black heart, hardened and dirty. Its pulse was sporadic and labored. It seemed to be pumping a thick black oily liquid, which was somehow killing the heart. Then, in came a tractor—a pink plastic tractor!

I know that bit sounds crazy, but at that age I had a plastic toy tractor, which was pink, that I used to play with. It was the same tractor I saw in the vision. As the tractor came in it took away the dirty old heart and brought in a clean fresh heart, which was full of life and beating at a good steady pace. I also saw Jesus. I knew it was Jesus even though I had never seen Him before. He did not look like the handsome, pristine, longhaired man wearing a white robe and blue sash I had seen in all the drawings in my children's Bible. He was real, a real man. He looked rugged, His face scarred and worn, and His robes were grey in colour and the hem and His feet were in need of a wash.

His feet attracted me first. Though they were dirty, and His sandals worn and tatty, I saw in His feet the nail holes, marks of His crucifixion. His hair was long and His beard slightly unkempt. His eyes, blue like sapphires, were deep and full of such wisdom. Kindness and gentleness shined forth from His eyes. There in that tent as I lay on the floor, Jesus knelt beside me and stroked my hair as I lay silent with my eyes closed yet still seeing Him. I felt His gentle touch and His compassion. I felt peace as tears rolled down His face as He looked at me, and I knew His heart was filled with compassion for me. I felt His tears drop from His face and land on mine. His nail-scarred hand reached out and slipped nicely into my clenched fist, and He held my hand. I lay there and allowed the warmth of His gentle care to surround me.

I don't know how long I lay there, but almost as though I knew it was time, when I was ready, my eyes slowly began to open and I sat up.

I looked around and did not see Jesus. I worried for a second that I had been dreaming and making it up, but then I felt a soft burning sensation in my hands, still clenched, and I knew then that Jesus was there holding my hands. I looked up to the celling of the tent and saw only the canvas roof. The open heavens I had seen earlier were gone. It was tempting at that moment to be sad for what was no longer there or even to deny what I had just experienced. That would have been easy as I looked around and saw that nobody was focusing on me when I began to stand again, peace still filled me and I felt an overwhelming sense of joy.

Holy Spirit was moving, and He was taking half the tent with His wave of love, peace, and compassion. Nobody really noticed a tiny 6-year-old girl and whether she had fallen. It would have been easy to return to my parents and deny the experience I just had with Jesus and God's beautiful Holy Spirit, and for a moment that thought crossed my mind. I knew, however, that something had changed in me that day, and I knew there would be no way I would want to deny what wondrous love I had experienced. Upon returning to the place where my family and our church were camping, I took no time in declaring that I had seen God and that God had made me fall.

My parents where no longer skeptical because my Dad had his own encounter with Holy Spirit that day. As a child I did not understand how important it was that my parents accepted what I was saying about my encounter with Holy Spirit. As I have grown older, though, I have become saddened by adults who are often too quick to declare that children cannot move in the wondrous ways of the Spirit. That is *not* true. In fact, children are often more open to a true relationship with Holy Spirit, which is why God bids us to have a childlike faith. I now understand how beautiful it was that my parents accepted and understood that a child could have such a rich and real encounter with Holy Spirit. Now in my 20s I hunger after that beautiful childlike faith in Holy Spirit that I used to have.

Though Holy Spirit showed His power to me that week, something even more special happened to me, an encounter even more beautiful. There is a very special place to me in that showground in Shepton Mallet. A stream runs right through the showground, and there is a place where an old stone bridge arcs over the stream, and it was there where in 1994 I met my Lord and Saviour.

I don't know how much knowledge of Jesus I had at that point in my life. I knew the Bible stories from Sunday school, but I am not sure I really knew them to be real in my heart. What I was experiencing during those few days that year, however, was very real and I did not question it.

I did not know that some people did not *see* Jesus. As I sat by that stone bridge the day after my Heavenly encounter in the children's tent, I saw a man. He was the same man I had seen as I lay there with my eyes shut, the man I had known to be Jesus. Only this time I wasn't lying down and my eyes were not shut. As I said before, He was not beautiful in any outward way, but He was what I used to call a "glowing person". There are people in this world who literally shine God. I called them glowing people. Jesus was the ultimate glowing person. I had never seen anyone more glowing than He. Although I knew He was Jesus, I did not consider this to be unusual. He looked at me and smiled a warm smile with His beautiful blue eyes smiling along with His mouth and He waved. I smiled and waved back.

I was standing on the bridge looking at the stream, which wound away from me behind some trees. Jesus was standing in the water just beside the trees. As a 6-year-old I saw nothing odd about this or wrong with that scenario. I watched Him play with fish, every kind of fish, thay looked as bright and as colourful as tropical fish in the Caribbean. It seemed He was trying to catch them with His hands yet never seemed to get them, and water was splashing everywhere. He made me laugh. It was a real laugh, a happy laugh, at a time when I had felt that I was forgetting how to laugh. I asked what He was doing, and He told me He was playing with the fish. I remember telling Him that I didn't think the fish wanted to play. Jesus laughed and agreed. Then He was gone, and so were the fish.

My encounter with Jesus that day was the first of many. A few years later while I was at a Christian

Bible week in Northern Ireland, I had a vision from Jesus in which He was again in a river playing with fish, and He invited me to play with Him. I love fish. Fish remind me so much of Jesus that I keep fish in a tank at home now and enjoy watching them while I pray or worship. I saw the holes in His hands while He played in the stream, and for some reason I grew to trust those holes.

As the weeks and months went on, I kept seeing Jesus and feeling His warmth. He never really said anything; I just saw Him. I also had more and more encounters with Holy Spirit. It never dawned on me that some would consider this move of God as false or at best childish imagination. It was God. I knew of nothing else I could compare my encounter with God to. Though at times in my life I have wondered if this was simply my imagination, as I have grown to understand prophecy and the way in which God talks to us, I know for certain that it was real.

As the years passed, however, my life seemed to slip more and more into despair. I felt as though I had lost joy and peace, and worry and sadness began to consume me. I didn't know why, but I could not seem to make myself feel anything good. The bullying in school just got worse as the years rolled by. I never told anyone—not even my parents, and I grew to hate myself for letting the bullies get to me and for not telling anybody sooner. I don't know why I never told my parents. I was not afraid of telling them, I just never did, it's something I cannot explain. It was my sister who told them in the end.

I have never not had faith. I have never not known God and never not believed in Him. I have struggled, however, and I have questioned who I am. I have questioned what the purpose of life is. I have wrestled with too many questions and wondered if I would ever be free, but I have never doubted or blamed God. As somebody who has always known Holy Spirit, I have often wondered why life wasn't always as easy and as simple as it could have been. I have walked on the edge of life never quite getting to where I wanted to be until I made a choice, a choice to be free.

Freedom from our pain, guilt, and anger is a choice. It is a difficult choice and a hard path to walk down, but it *is* a choice. Jesus hung naked on a cross, tortured and humiliated for my freedom and your freedom. The work has been done, the price paid. Being free does not require that you have an encounter with Holy Spirit or Jesus the way I have. It does not require that split-second Damascus Road experience that we all hear about in those testimonies at church. Nor does it require that you experienced the Toronto Blessing or met God at a young age. It is about being real, embracing the journey, and making a choice. It is about growing an intimate relationship with God. Galatians 5:1 says, "it is for freedom that Christ has set us free". We in the church throw around such words as "being free" or "being saved," and yet we only very rarely explain what they mean. Sadly, I have met a number of people who have been in the church for many years and who know God and the Bible very well and yet miss the point entirely. They do not know what it is to be free. They live a half-life not realising the wonderful gift of freedom they have as believers.

A woman who used to minister deeply to my brokenness once told me that she spends hours of her time correcting people's theology and their ideas of themselves and of who God is and who He is in their lives. Though it is so sad whenever there is brokenness and pain, it is an even sadder thing when we are talking about Christian brokenness. We as believers have the Spirit of God within us, which means that God resides in us. We have the power of God moving in us. The enemy will lie to keep us trapped and tell us we are not free and can *never* be free—that it is impossible. When we Christians face hardship we often ask, "Where is God? Isn't He supposed to protect me?" As a believer from the age of 6, I wondered, "Shouldn't God be there to stop the bullies?" That is different to blame, but it could very easily become blame. satan will use those thoughts and that is when things begin to feel impossible. That is when we often ask, "If He didn't stop it was He there? And if He wasn't there then how do we know He is there now?"

While I agree that it is impossible ever to be completely free from the pains of this world and that we will never fully realise freedom from the harshness of the world till we go to Heaven, I am convinced that it is sad—even tragic—for us not to live in the life Christ died for us to have here on Earth simply because we are just waiting for the life He promised for us *after* death. The Kingdom of God is here and now. Jesus did not die just to secure our place in Heaven. He died and rose again to bring Heaven to Earth and to defeat satan. He died so that mankind could live in intimate relationship with God here on this Earth now, and forever in Heaven after we die.

This book is not my testimony as such. Rather, it is the story of how I, that tiny 6-year-old who encountered Holy Spirit in 1994, grew up to live a life full of hurt and brokenness in a bitter, angry darkness and yet was able to find a place of freedom from that darkness. I was able to make choices that could bring me out of the darkness in which I found myself. Jesus has given us the tools to stop feeling like the walking dead.

There is hope, there is a future, and it is possible to know good and Godly joy. Freedom from pain and from our past is possible. We can stand shoulder to shoulder with Jesus and face what seems impossible to face. I do not deny suffering or that Jesus appears at times to do nothing to relieve it (and in fact appears to make it worse), but I do know one thing: Jesus Christ died for our freedom and He beat death on the cross. Though I do not have all the answers, I do share the journey and path that I followed and the choices I made, and I know that the wrong and bad choices I made lead to death whereas the right and good choices I made lead to life.

In Deuteronomy 30:19 God said:

"I have set before you life and death, blessings and curses, now choose life so that you and your children may live."

I choose life...

CHAPTER TWO

GOD'S WAY

Choose life. What does that mean? How can we choose life? We are alive and then one day we die. That is the natural order of things. How then can we choose life? When talking about choosing life, I am not talking about physical life and death but rather about spiritual life and death. There are two powers, satan and God. There is the physical realm and the spiritual realm. The physical realm is what we see and feel and the Earth we live on. The spiritual realm is the Heavenly realm, the things we do not see, Heaven and hell. In the spiritual realm a battle is raging between those two powers.

As I stated earlier, God is more powerful than satan. There is no dispute about that. God is sovereign and all-powerful. God knows He is more powerful and satan knows God is more powerful, but do you know it? I mean *really* know it? satan longs to be more powerful than God. He longs to overcome God and is thus fighting for you and for your life. Spiritual death is separation from God. Sin separates us from God, and sin is death. God never stops caring about us. He never stops loving us. He never turns His back on us, not even when we sin.

Sin is choosing to say or do something that is not of God and that God would not want for our lives. When we sin we are telling God that we believe satan is more powerful and that we choose his ways. Every sin is in some way saying that satan is more interesting, more powerful, more beautiful, more fun, or more capable of saving than God. For example, if somebody drinks too much and constantly gets drunk just to fit in with their peers, that sin is saying that the person God created is not good enough to fit in. Thus, instead of praying and asking God to help them make good friends they are saying that satan and his ways are more capable of helping them make friends. So when we sin, we turn our backs on God and say that for whatever reason we prefer satan's way. We turn away from God; He *never* turns away from us. The wonderful thing is that we can turn back to Him because of Jesus and His act of love on the cross. God is always there waiting and longing for us to turn back to Him, for there is no guilt or condemnation because we are in Christ. We can always turn back to God, He is always there waiting to accept us.

From reading the Bible, we know in our heads that God is bigger and more powerful, but do we know it in our hearts? Do we know it in our lives? Do we know it in our very being? If we do know it, do we live as though we do? Though I have always known that God is bigger than satan, I have certainly not always lived in it as though I know it. satan wants to rob, kill, and destroy us (John 10:10). satan wants to separate us from God and destroy our the intimate relationship with God that God intended for us. That is the spiritual battle. satan is not fighting for the souls of us believers in hell after we die because he knows that our salvation is secure. If we accept and believe in Jesus as our Saviour, we will be secure in Heaven after we die. satan has no say about what happens to us *after* we die, but he is trying to rob us of our freedom before we die.

satans mission is to prevent us from enjoying life in beautiful intimacy with God now—here on Earth. he does not want us to be free from his bondage and brokenness. If he cannot deprive us of our salvation and consign us to hell forever, he will do all he can to destroy our life and rob us of our relationship with God our Father. That is why we do not always live in the freedom and assurance we could while we are alive. This is what we call brokenness. Christian brokenness is different to secular brokenness simply because of God. As Christians we have the authority and freedom in Christ to live deep and truly free lives in Him if only we choose to or know how to choose to live in such wonderful freedom from satan's ways. To choose that freedom is what I mean when I say that we can choose life.

I know that the church is often very quick to teach freedom ministry and teach that God heals, which of course He does, yet we shy away from the question that comes from the fact that He does not always choose to heal or restore in the ways we want or expect or as quickly as we want or expect, and the church does not always have answer to that. That is the problem with suffering, pain, sickness, and death. It begs the questions, "Where is God when these things happen? If He stands in full authority over satan, why do these things happen?"

Those are big questions and before we can answer them, we must break it down. First, it is important to acknowledge that these things are real. Illness is real. Bondage, pain, suffering, and abuse are all real. They are roots—the deep-seated causes and circumstances—out of which sprout fear, shame, guilt, mistrust, anger, bitterness, and all those decaying mindsets that manifest in behaviours such as aggression: both verbal and physical, self-harm, substance abuse, eating disorders, lies, attention-seeking, and addictions and so much more. These things happen. They are difficult and they are real.

They are not right and they are not fair. They are *not* what God wants for us or for His world. We must begin with the belief that God is good, because He is. God is good. When we don't understand the true goodness of God, we begin to think that God might have been in some way involved in or part of our difficulty. Then we don't just ask "Where was God?" but begin to think that He caused our pain. Then we ask, "Why did God do this to me?" If we in any way, even in a tiny way, think that God can be in any way responsible for our suffering and difficulties, then how can we expect Him or trust Him to heal us or save us from them? So let's affirm that God is good—entirely good. He is not responsible for our pain. satan has corrupted the world and brought pain and death and decay. satan—not God—is responsible for your suffering, pain, and sickness. It is very important that we are clear on this in our minds. When looking at our suffering, we need to know and understand who God is.

How we respond to suffering is what's really important. God is not to blame for our suffering or our mistakes. God did not say that we Christians would not suffer in this world. He did not say we would not have pain. And although we are not immune to the pain and trials of the world, we have a God who is greater than the world. We are in the world but not of the world because we are of God. "The One who is in you is greater than the one that is in the world" (1 John 4:4).

There is a consequence to every action we as humans take, whether good or bad, that results in either a good or a bad consequence. That seems fair until we think hard about it...

The real hard crux of the matter is that sometimes we face the consequences of somebody else's actions. Take abuse, for example. The effects of abuse on a person's body and mind—that is, physical and spiritual well-being—is a direct consequence of the actions of the abuser not the actions of the survivor, and yet the survivor is the one who is left to suffer. In other cases, we can suffer the consequences of things that we have no control over or the actions of others that we know nothing about.

For example, a few years ago I had the great privilege of meeting a beautiful, gentle woman of God and celebrating her 102nd birthday with her and her family. Though she said little, she radiated the love of God even though her granddaughter, who she loved very dearly, was not at the birthday celebrations because she had died at 47 years old.

That beautiful woman of God felt the pain of loss for her granddaughter at the same time she celebrated her 102nd birthday. There are some things in this world that do not make sense to us and that do not seem right. That beautiful woman of God has recently gone home to be with the Lord at 105 years old and will see her granddaughter again in Heaven. Or another example is the natural disasters that have rocked the world killing many in recent years. Tragedies happen, and the reality is, there is no answer for them. We cannot pretend otherwise. We cannot try to reason out or understand why those things happen. The only answer is that Jesus restores, Jesus heals the broken hearts and shattered dreams. If we stand shoulder to shoulder with Jesus in our times of trouble then we can survive any situation in this life. I am not saying it will be easy. Jesus did not promise it would be easy only that He would be there.

One of the prevailing problems for Christians in our day is that people expect to be able to understand and explain everything. They expect an answer. They don't like hard work or long-term solutions and don't want to wait for slow change. If they do not get a quick fix or immediate answer, they will give up and say it didn't work or there was no point to it. Those who are ready and willing to embark on the journey, however, slowly but surely advancing towards the prize, will discover freedom, a deeper revelation of who Christ is, and a peace and a joy beyond anything they have ever imagined.

I hope and pray that the tools I share with you from my journey will empower you along the way. I pray that Jesus will lead and guide you to places far beyond your imagination. I pray that you will come to know true freedom and be set free from all that has bound you. I pray that the gentle Lord Jesus will meet you in your place of confusion, worry, and shame and minister to you in the way that only He can. I pray that in your praising and in your joy Jesus will praise with you. I pray that in your gladness Jesus will be glad with you and that in your freedom you will experience even more freedom and wholeness through continuing to walk with Him.

We are all on the journey to freedom. It will not be over until we are in Heaven. It is true that some people live a freer life than others. When I used to walk around in a half-life state, I felt as though I was waiting to die. I didn't know how to survive beyond simply waiting to die. It has been quite a journey for me—at times a long, hard journey, a journey that seemed impossible, and many times I questioned whether this would work. I wondered if I would ever be free from the terrible feelings and emptiness I felt. I have all too often questioned whether it would have been easier to give in and give up rather than try to believe in the possibility that I could feel anything other than the pain and confused emptiness I had felt for so long. When I started out on my journey of healing, it seemed so impossible that I would find healing and peace. I often wondered if it would not be easier just to give up and accept being broken and hurting than to try to find freedom and not get free and thus end up feeling like a failure.

Whenever I am thinking like that, I know that I must turn to God in prayer. I affirm that I must never give up, for God has a wonderful plan for my life and longs to see me free and living out His plan. He has a plan for your life also. Though at times you may doubt that you will ever reach God's plan for your life, you must not give up, even if it seems impossible, because God will never leave you, and the healing and peace will make the journey with all its challenges worthwhile.

I know that when you are in the thick of pain and anguish and brokenness the last thing you want to hear is that it is a choice to get out that pain and hurt … but it is true. I am not saying it in just a "get over it" kind of way. What I am saying is that Jesus has lovingly given us tools to live in the full abundance that He died for us to have. We have a choice—to do the right thing or the wrong thing. To be healed and set free, we must choose to live God's way. But we could choose to live satan's way. The choice between the two is sometimes a very difficult one. Do not be disheartened or annoyed with yourself because every single one of us from time to time does something we regret. There have been times in my life when I have regretted things daily. Remember that a journey is about the traveling not the destination. We can reach the ultimate goal of freedom only when we are in Heaven, but because of Jesus' work on the cross when we do slip up we can turn back to God, be restored, and there is no guilt. Enjoy the exciting journey of getting to know God more and coming into a deeper revelation of healed freedom.

If you are reading this book, you are already on your way, for you have already made a choice, a choice to read this book. For some of you, choosing to read a book like this is a big step. It could mean that you are admitting that there is something in you, maybe deep down and long forgotten, that needs healing and God's loving touch. If so, let me tell you how amazing you are. The fact that you have at least in a small way chosen to admit what can be a very hard thing to admit—that something is not right and that you need help—is beautiful and brave and honouring to God. I pray that God meets you in your need somehow through reading this book and you will continue to grow deeper and deeper in your relationship with Him.

If you have already been walking in freedom, maybe for a long time now or maybe for just a short while, I pray that this book will be a refresher for your soul and that you will continue to grow deeper in your journey to freedom with God that will be complete only when you reach Heaven and meet Him face to face.

If you are not really sure why you are reading this book, maybe God led you to it or a friend lent it to you for some reason, I pray God's blessing on you as you choose to read this book. May you find and continue to find freedom and love with Jesus and may the loving Lord Jesus meet you today.

CHAPTER THREE

A PRAYER WARRIOR

I don't know of any human way to truly overcome our pains, our brokenness, and our struggles. The only answer I have to pain and trauma is Jesus Christ. Because of what Jesus Christ did on the cross Holy Spirit restores and heals us. We know God as a Father, a good and perfect Father who loves His children, a Father who is good and *only* good. We know Jesus as the Son. Jesus came to earth 2,000 years ago and walked this earth as a man. He was a good man who only did good things. He was fully human and yet fully God. He came down from Heaven for one reason, one purpose—to restore and renew mankind's relationship with God by saving mankind from satan and the death and decay that satan brings to the world. Jesus' heart was so filled with compassion for mankind that He willingly died in the most agonizing and humiliating way to defeat death by dying and then rising again three days later. Jesus had the power to save Himself but choose not to. In doing so He defeated satan so that satan has no claim on or authority over our lives. It is because of Jesus' sacrificial death, we can be healed and restored from all pain and brokenness that comes from satan. Only through Jesus we can be restored.

Holy Spirit is the third part of the divine trinity. He is the One people know less about. He is the most mysterious member of the Trinity. Yet He is so beautiful, so powerful, and so ever-present. When people talk of *feeling* God, they are talking of Holy Spirit. He is a personable being. He is completely whole and completely divine. He is the glory of God and the power of God. He comes like a gentleman waiting to be invited, and yet He comes crashing into our lives with such force and power that we cannot deny Him. He can move mountains. He is the power that raised Christ from the dead. He is the almighty Shekhinah glory of God.

Holy Spirit is often described as a wind or a fire. He is neither and yet He is both. He is a great mystery, and yet He is always with us. He is a Wonderful Counsellor. He is for all believers. He is the seal of our salvation (Ephesians 1:13). When you accept the gift of salvation, Holy Spirit seals that salvation within you. He is that still small voice and He is that deep conviction. He declares salvation into you, and His authority and power resides in you. "The One who is in you is greater than the one who is in the world" (1 John 4:4).

So many Christians do not know or understand what great power resides within them; many do not know the authority over life and death they have in their grip. Believers can make a choice that can bring them into beautiful freedom and wholeness.

As a believer you are in Christ. This means that by choosing to accept Jesus we come into Him restored in a new identity. We cannot come to God in our sinful nature, so Jesus died on the cross taking our sinful nature so that we could come to God in Him. People sometimes take this to mean that we somehow hide in Jesus so that all God sees when He looks at us is Jesus—almost as if we are objects placed inside a box and covered with a lid so that God only sees the box instead of the object inside. It isn't like that. Jesus literally transforms us to become more like Him. God looks at us and still sees us. God wants to see us because He delights in us. As we grow deeper in our relationship with Jesus, we are transformed to become more and more like Him.

This is not a rose-tinted fairy tale. This is not me trying to convince you that once you are in Christ you will not have trials and pain—you will. Being a Christian does not make life good and perfect, and in fact can make it worse, but it is a real life, a beautifully freeing life. My life has not been easy because I am a Christian. At times in my life I have faced trials as a direct result of being a Christian.

We are in the world but Jesus said that like Him we are not *of* the world (John 17:16) and "in this world you will have trouble. But take heart! I have overcome the world." (John 16:33). This is the beautiful reality of what a life restored means, that even though we face trials Jesus has overcome them and so now we can be in intimate relationship with Him.

Living in that intimate relationship with God is how He intended us to live with Him. As with any other relationship, we must grow and nurture our relationship with God. It took me many years to understand what that intimate relationship looks like. So often we tend to measure God against our earthly relationships. We confine God's love in what we understand or experience of love, and that experience is not always good. We often find ourselves measuring God against our earthly standards, which is understandable because that is what we know. When people ask me who Jesus is to me, I describe Him as my best friend, my first love even though I know I have not always lived as though He is my best friend or my first love.

Those are big claims for me to make, and as I look at the friendships I enjoy and all the people and things I love, I question whether I can really say He is my best friend or my first love? Many of us consider the people and things we love and ask, "Where does God fit into that?" That is often a hard question to ask ourselves.

Often I cannot say truly that He is my first love. I have love for my family and my friendships. I have love for the things I own. I have love for hot chocolate, which truly is the best drink in the world, and I have love for sausages. Love for these sorts of things is not wrong. We are made as relational beings, and God has made wonderful things in the world for us to enjoy. He made each of us with our own likes and dislikes. I know many people who do not like sausages, but I love them so much! The fact that we all like different things makes life exciting. It would be boring if we all liked the same thing. The question is not what we like; the question really is: "Does your love for God come before all these things?"

When I was younger my youth leader told me she loved God more than she loved her husband. That really shocked me, and I didn't understand it because I had always thought a person was supposed to love their husband or wife more than anybody or anything. I remember very distinctly telling that youth leader that I thought that probably made her a bad wife. Now I see how wonderfully beautiful her faith was and also how wonderfully beautiful her marriage was.

If we can put God first, as our first love before anything and before any relationship, we will not only grow deeper in our relationship with God and grow in intimacy with Him but we will grow deeper in our relationships with others.

Until we know and move in the love of God, we cannot truly love others. We can only love as we have first been loved (1 John 4:19). That is a difficult verse and one that many people wrestle with. Many people do not feel loved and do not see or understand God's love for them. And the underlying issue is that it is impossible to truly love others if we do not know the love of God.

For a long time I hated that verse in the Bible—"We love because He first loved us" (1 John 4:19)—because I felt as though I had loved people even when I had not felt or understood or experienced God's love for myself. But I have come to understand that verse to be true. Now having had a true love encounter with Jesus myself I have come to understand that unless you have known what God's love is and felt it for yourself you cannot truly love another.

Our relationship with Jesus can be very beautiful and very special. Like all relationships, our relationship with Jesus is individual to each person and needs to be grown and developed over time and interaction. We are not expected to trust Jesus right away. All too often I hear those in the church tell others to "trust in Jesus". That really annoys me because how can a person trust Him if they do not really know Him? I would not expect anyone to trust me upon first meeting me. I would not expect somebody to trust me until we had built a relationship. Trust is earned.

When I was struggling with the heavy weight of guilt over the bad choices I had made a few years back, I knew that only Jesus was going to set me free from the tremendous guilt I was carrying. I did not want fear and shame to keep me trapped any longer. I have also felt great shame and guilt for the choices of others that have affected me, but only Jesus can and has set me free. It is important to grow a relationship with Jesus. We do this through prayer.

Prayer is about a secure, confident, rich, and perfect relationship with God. That beautiful, perfect, and intimate relationship with God that He intended for us needs to be developed and grown over time. Prayer is communicating with God, which is what we were made to experience. In Genesis we read about Adam walking intimately with God in the Garden. We were created to walk intimately with Him. When satan tempted Eve corruption and sin entered the world. Prayer is about developing that closeness again.

When I was beginning to pray and meet with Jesus as I was coming out of some deep, dark years, I began to think about the things I did with my friends—how I spent my time with my friends. I wondered how was I supposed to spend time with Jesus. Because I had grown up in the church, in some way prayer had always been a part of my life, but I didn't really know how to pray or even why. I had become so used to praying only when I needed Jesus or when I needed something that I forgot it was supposed to be about a relationship with Him. Jesus had been my very real companion in my darkest years. I used to see Jesus sitting next to me most days, and yet somehow I forgot that Jesus was a friend. I forgot He is God and that He knew all things. I forgot He is perfect love.

When prayer is part of your upbringing or you've been in the habit of it for a while it becomes far too easy for it to become something you do, something that is just part of you. It is just a routine part of your life, and you do not think it through.

As a child I learned that prayer is talking to Jesus. I am not sure anyone ever told me that He talks back to us. I did not grow up expecting Jesus to talk to me. I knew He could because sometimes He did, but it was not something I was taught to expect in every prayer. Yet in conversations with our friends we don't just talk at them and not expect them to talk back to us. If we come to faith later in life, especially from a place of brokenness, we are taught to speak to Jesus and might be taught that He speaks back to us because He loves us, but we are rarely taught to build a relationship. Yet that relationship is where we find healing and grow into the healing. It is through developing a deep prayer life that we begin to choose to live the life Christ died for us to have.

If you are unsure how to pray just start simple, start by saying "hello" to Jesus. Tell Him how you day was. Tell Him what you think you are going to do in the next few days. It is in prayer that you start to fight against satan. It is in prayer that you begin to learn to hear Jesus and slowly over time as you wait for His ansers and let Him talk back to you, you will begin to trust Him and that intimate relationship will begin to be built. It is prayer that is the biggest weapon against satan because it aligns yourself with

God as you begin to build a closeness to Him, the very thing satan want's to destroy.

Though each person will build a relationship with Jesus in a unique way, it always starts with prayer. It starts with reading about Jesus. Do not be afraid to ask Jesus to respond to your prayers. As you spend time listening to Jesus, you will find that He talks back. He cares about you and your life. He will respond, and you can tell Him about the things you like, about your pains, and about your life. It doesn't matter that He already knows, He delights in hearing it from you.

Your pain has a voice. Jesus is okay with that. Your pain has a voice that needs to speak out. That voice might be angry. That voice might be broken or filled with tears. That's okay. Jesus wants to hear your voice. He wants to hear your pain. Never bottle up your pain. If your pain is raging mad, let your voice come. Scream if you need to scream. Blame God if you need to blame God, He is okay with that. He cares about your feelings. Let the voice of your pain speak out. At this point in your journey to healing and choosing life in Christ, it is important that you allow yourself to give voice to your feelings. Give voice to your pain and give voice to your anger.

Let Jesus minister His gentle love into the voice of

your pain. By allowing the voice of your pain to speak out to Jesus, you are letting Him minister to you. That is the start of what it means to choose life.

CHAPTER FOUR

WHO AM I?

As I looked through a large box of old photographs, which had been cluttering my room for years, I was met with reminders of times long since forgotten. A wealth of memories that I once thought I would never want to forget, now haphazardly stuffed in a big brown box, awaiting the day I would find myself free enough from my busy lifestyle to sort through them. Images, recorded living moments stopped in time, there forever. A memory captured, a moment of who I was, of my past. So many individual moments.

When I was 16 I bought my very own first digital camera and found suddenly that I was not limited to 24 hazy shots on a roll that would be printed 6x4" no matter whether it was a good shot or not. I found that I could now document every second of the world around me and forever stop that moment in time. I could then upload all the pictures to the computer, pick out the best ones among the hundreds and hundreds and store them by the hundreds on a CD and have the best ones printed at the chemist. I would then blue-tack them up on my bedroom wall, hundreds of photographs covering the walls documenting happy times with friends.

As the years rolled by, however, and my life moved on from those teenage college friends, I took the photographs down. They now remained stored only on CDs that were never looked at and on the print-outs stuffed in a box, forgotten and collecting dust. There I sat more than 10 years on from the day I got my first digital camera with tears streaming down my cheeks as I remembered long-forgotten times— times when I seemed for that moment at least so happy, so lively, and so unaware of the world at large around of me.

It was at that moment that I came across a photograph of 30 teenagers, a drama group from a performing arts college diploma huddled together at centre stage of the theatre. Each one was fighting for the attention of the camera, each in their own way trying to stand out and be noticed, each hoping to be "the next big thing", reaching for the goal of fame. My eyes moved past them, however, as I found myself drawn to one solitary figure standing at the back and to the far left of the group, rigid, arms folded, body posture closed. The body language was saying so clearly, "I don't want to be here", echoed by a faint smile and a look of uncomfortable fear in the deep brown eyes.

I stared at that figure in the photograph for a long time ... so out of place from the group at large, so *not* wanting to be in the spotlight, so timid and quiet and desperate to slip away into the background unnoticed by her peers. And yet in her own way she was so loud, so noticeable, and so obvious, so very different from the others that the eyes could not help but be drawn to her. Her hair, so fluorescent pink that it almost glowed off the photograph, was cut in the unusual short spiked style with a long straight fringe that almost covered the entire left side of her face. Her eye make-up was bright and colourful with a pink silvery splatter along the cheekbone, and thick black eyeliner above and below both eyes swirled into curly patterns on each side of the face.

The clothes screamed for attention, too, looking as though they had come straight out of the 1960s hippie scene with a flash of a 90s rave. A bright-blue poncho covering a purple top, sleeveless only on one arm. A horrendously bright-pink miniskirt hung awkwardly around the waist. Bright-turquoise leggings clung tightly to her legs, red-and-white-striped socks could just be seen crawling up the legs with big pink furry boots looking like fluffy animals on both feet.

The young woman was so awkwardly out of place wishing nobody could see her and yet so obvious in her splash of colour, so obviously standing out from the group. Looking at the photograph, I sat back in my chair and smiled at the 16-year-old me. That one photograph was so telling and yet gave away nothing of the real me who was for some confused unknown reason trapped, broken, hurting, and bitter behind that pink hair.

I was that same 16-year-old who was attending a church youth group at the time. It was there when I heard the verse Isaiah 61:3: "to bestow on them a crown of beauty instead of ashes, the oil of joy instead of mourning and a garment of praise instead of a spirit of despair". This verse was intended to encourage, build up, and edify the hurting and broken-hearted. Most who hear this verse feel at peace and expectant for their future. When I heard that verse, however, I hated it. It did not liberate me. It did not build me up or encourage me. It angered me and frightened me. Even though I had been a Christian most of my life, I did not feel free and I did not feel as close to God as I would have liked to be. I was living with that spirit of despair. I was in mourning and in a pit of ashes. I had a very low self-image and did not like who I was. I didn't like what I looked like, and I felt that being a Christian did not help because I felt that as a Christian I was *meant* to feel good, to feel joy, to feel secure, and to feel God loved me.

But none of that was there for me or right for me. None of that had sunk in with me or felt real to me. I did not feel as though I could match up to the image of a perfect Christian that I had created in my mind. So it was very hard to hear that God had given me a crown of beauty and the oil of joy, and I did not like it at all. It just didn't make sense to me, and I could not make it make sense. I found it so confusing. I felt like there was a certain shape or mould of how it was to be a Christian, and I couldn't make myself fit into it or conform to it. I began to feel trapped in a deep, horrid feeling of never quite fitting in, which led to a weary feeling of brokenness. I didn't feel free, and it did not feel very liberating to be a Christian. My faith added to my feeling of being trapped because I felt as though I could never live up to the expectations I thought the church had for me.

Yet I knew that as a Christian I was somehow supposed to be free because Jesus had died for me to be free. I felt I could never be what God wanted me to be because I felt a deep-rooted pain and could never explain where it had come from. I could not make myself feel as though I was doing what God wanted of me because in truth I had a very distorted idea of what God wanted me. I had tried to feel free. I thought freedom was something I was supposed to work harder at and something I was supposed to strive to have. I tried so hard to feel how I thought I was supposed to feel as a Christian, but somehow I did not quite feel as though I was free no matter how hard I tried. I was never free from feeling trapped and broken, never free from feeling controlled by my own bad thoughts and emotions. I could never find that garment of praise. Instead, there just seemed to be an overwhelming nothingness.

I felt that I must have done something wrong, that I must have been wrong. I was not fitting in the church, and yet that did not seem any different from any other area of my life. I had never really felt the sense of belonging that I was so desperately seeking. I would have loved it if I could have taken some kind of medicine that made everything all right again in an instant. I would have loved it if there were a simple prayer I could have been told to pray and then by some holy act or miracle things would have changed for me in an instant. But that is not the way it works. It really was a process of learning over time the subtlety of truth and lies. It was a process and a journey, a journey I am still on and that will not end until the day I die.

Yet as I look back at the 16-year-old me and remember who I once was and where I have come from, I smile. What I had not understood when I first read that verse from Isaiah is that the miracle I so desperately longed for had already been performed. Christ had already come and set me free. Galatians 5:1 says: that it was for freedom that Christ came to set me free. This means I had already been given that garment of praise, and that oil of joy was set before me. I already had that crown of beauty, but I didn't know it. Those things were already won for me when Christ hung naked on the cross for me. I did not have to strive in the way I had been striving for my freedom.

What I did not understand was that I had a choice—to live in that or not. I could choose truth or lies, blessings or curses, as it says in Deuteronomy 30:19. I had to learn to choose to accept that Christ had actually died for me. The fact is, the Bible is true, and the Bible says that Jesus died to set us free. Yet the problem for so many people is that we do not believe it. We find it easier to believe what satan tells us in the world than what God tells us through His Word in the Bible. I need to tell you something very important: Freedom is already yours, and life is in your grasp! It is a matter of choosing to believe, of choosing that it is real. I know that many of us cannot believe without seeing.

The evidence of Christ's work in my life is before me in that small photograph taken when I was 16. Sometimes we need to be reminded of who we used to be before we can see the good God has done in our lives. I often think God hasn't done much in me, but as I look at that photograph I *know* God has done great work in me. It is not easy. In fact, it is a very difficult road of constant choice, but it is so rewarding and so liberating. Freedom is possible. Joy is available. And there will be beauty out of the ashes. I used to be a very hurt person, and in my pain and hurt I hurt others. I have lied and manipulated others in the past trying to get my own needs to feel loved and cared for met. I am not proud of those things, but nor do I deny them. These things make up who I am today, and to look back on that shy and quiet young woman who thought she could manipulate her way to love and freedom helps me know that the tools for life's success that Jesus gave me and that I chose to use have set me free, and the evidence continues to live on in who I am.

As a teenager I, like most teenagers, was really trying to find my place in the world. I would wrestle over question after question, pain after pain. I longed for answers to the rejection, pain, and self-loathing I was feeling. I had encountered such terrible bullying when I was a young child, and I was desperate to fit in. Yet I just could not seem to fit in no matter what or how hard I tried. I hated who I thought I was and because of that I longed to know why God had created me and who I was supposed to be. If God had a purpose for everything He made and God didn't make mistakes, then there must have been some reason for me and for me to be the way I was because I could not seem to make myself like the way I was or who I was.

At that point I began to really question who we human beings truly are? How were we designed? Who were we created to be? These are the age-old questions that have plagued mankind for many generations. For eons, humans have asked the question "who am I?" and many philosophers old and new have attempted to find a satisfying answer to that burning question. As I look at the world around me, I see a culture that is so bound and so obsessed with feeling good about itself. Although we rarely realise it, the *who am I?* question has become a bit of a modern obsession. It is so subtle in the way we look to define ourselves that often we define who we are and who we think we are without even realising what we are doing or why. Our culture has tried to find the answers to the *who am I?* question in worldly places, places that are not Godly, and now our society has taught us to become preoccupied with feeling good about ourselves. Because the culture gives us carefully defined notions of how feeling good about ourselves should look and thus we rarely turn to God to define us.

TV shows, song lyrics, magazines, celebrities, advertising, and social media all have a lot to say about self-image and how we should be, look, and act. It is simply everywhere. A person today in western society is apt to look to the world's idea of beauty, which put another way is the world's idea of how we can feel good about ourselves, in other word's satan's definition of good. Often this message is communicated in very subtle and sly ways. For example, in advertising we are told to buy this deodorant because it is the best, and how are we told that? Well, we see images of a young, well-built, muscular man spraying it on himself on a beach and then young, attractive woman come flocking to him. Basically we are not just sold a deodorant, we are sold an image that says if you buy this deodorant you will instantly be attractive to all these beautiful women. We are told that if we read a certain newspaper we will be more clever. We are shown images of a woman with long, thick, silky hair and subtly told that if only we buy a particular shampoo we will look like her—and who doesn't want to look like her?

We are sold an image alongside everything we buy. We are rarely sold just a product because the advertising campaigns are designed to make us feel inadequate in some way so that we will buy a product that can fill the gap and meet the need. Our TV shows are more and more only casting those who fit a specific pre-defined ideal of beauty in the leading roles, regardless of the person's acting ability and talent. Countless TV shows are devoted to making people over and changing their image to make them *look good*. Reality TV shows give ordinary people a grasp at fame, a fame that is hollow because as soon as we have a winner this year there's always next season and a new winner who will quickly follow. We are defined by what we look like, what we wear, what the celebrities wear, where we shop, who our partner is, how successful we are in our career, who our parents are, what their job is, where we live, whether we have kids, how successful they are, academic achievement, where we eat, what we eat, and so on. These things define us every day and play a big part in shaping our self-image. Yet God told us exactly who and what we are in His

Word, and we rarely bother look to God's Word for the truth about ourselves.

My heart breaks for the world. There is such a distorted notion of self-image out there as so many people are turning to the world's ways, to satan's ways, to define who they are.

The world cannot tell you how beautiful you are. The world cannot look at you and know that you are good the way that God—the God who made you and who knows you best and loves you most—knows you are good. The world cannot fulfill your needs and give you love. The world is hollow and empty and the world's beauty is fleeting. God's promises stand forever. God's truth shines out for all eternity. God is love and His love for you is never ending. You are beautiful, and only God's Word can truly tell you how stunningly beautiful you are. God can and will meet all your needs. He is there crying out, waiting for you, waiting for all of us. God longs for you to turn to Him to tell you how good you are.

God has called you beautiful.

CHAPTER FIVE

THE POWER OF WORDS

How we define and identify ourselves determines how we approach life. If I am what I do, I will always need to do more and achieve more to find my value. If I am what others say I am, I will always spend my time trying to please others to make them and myself happy instead of trying to please God. When I was a teenager I would be reading a magazine and see a model with long hair, big blue eyes, heavy make-up, and a skinny size-6 with rather large breasts. I looked in the mirror and saw none of that *beauty* in me.

I did not look to God's identity to define my standard for beautiful. My closest friend when I was a teenager is a wonderful woman. She was no more beautiful than I, though I thought she was. It was that she cared for herself, carried an inward beauty of positive thinking and friendliness. She would talk to people and have the confidence to give things a go in a positive way. She was kind and gentle and took time to listen to people instead of snap at them as I did. Those qualities are what shone through to make her liked and beautiful—even though she was thin and did have beautiful long brown hair. It wasn't her outward beauty but her inner beauty that made her attractive to others. She believed in herself and defined her identity in a positive way. I missed what made her beautiful and tired to make myself feel like I matched up to her outward beauty, yet never quite made it.

I was always thinking negatively and that is what shone through. I wore clothes that were too big and baggy, many layers of clothes, one over the other. I wore skirts over trousers to hide my thighs and waist and lots of make-up to try to cover up my face. After a while when that didn't seem to be working, I stopped wearing make-up and stopped caring for my appearance or trying to make myself beautiful. Believing I was ugly, I hung back out of the attention of others, and was shy and uninterested in social activities and the world around me. I let those labels of ugly, fat, immature, and many others take root in me, and I acted according to them. These labels that we put on ourselves or that others put on us really do stick, and it can take quite a while to rip them off.

It took many years before I was able to see myself as anything other than ugly and fat. I am not in any way saying there was any *one thing* that caused it, yet we are in a culture in which we are constantly seeing a certain idea of beautiful plastered everywhere we go. People over the years had called me ugly. Kids can be cruel, and I had been told so many times that I was ugly that it became a reality every time it was declared over me. I let it become my reality because I chose to accept it rather than accept and hear what those who loved me and cared about me said. Nor did I listen to God and what He said about the real me. I am not saying that I made a conscious choice to listen to the hurtful comments of others instead of God, but ultimately it was a choice nonetheless.

The power of words and the power of labels are so strong and can have a huge impact on our lives. This is why it is important to choose the words that you speak over yourself and over others wisely because they affect others and ourselves deeply and on a spiritual level. Words affect the world around you for the good or the bad. Words can hurt and tear down or they can heal and build up. How many of us have heard that saying, "Sticks and stones will break my bones but words and names will never hurt me"? I heard this when I was a child. We used to sing it as a clapping game in the playground, and it really bothered me. Words and names did hurt, *really* hurt. I was really badly bullied in primary school. I was called many names that for years afterwards I had to wrestle with. Words and names hurt!

I grew from those early primary school years to see myself as some kind of untouchable, an outcast like the lepers in the Bible, unclean. Words were really powerful, and yet I felt I was supposed to somehow not to allow them to hurt. I was supposed to stop them from hurting because this rhyme said that they wouldn't—that they would *never* hurt me. So then I began to label myself as weak because I would get upset when somebody said something hurtful about me. Those words took root, and I allowed myself to believe and wrap myself in those words. I was defined by what the bullies called me. It was declared so often over me that it became my reality.

Words are very powerful. I remember so clearly that one girl turned to me and said, "You are disgusting. Get away from me. Nobody wants you. Nobody likes you." Those words really hurt and really cut deep. At the time I was a bit upset, but I didn't really think the abuse affected me that much. It was quite normal for the others in my class to say these sorts of things, so I was not surprised to hear somebody say that sort of thing to me as I went to school each day.

That's just one example that I remember very clearly, probably because in some tiny way it can still bother me and affect me if I choose to let it.

Although it didn't surprise me, and although I expected it, deep down within me it caused so much hurt for so long, and I did let those words spoken over me day after day in primary school take root in me and they did hurt. Years later as I got older and was in high school I started to look back on those words, and before I realised it I had taken on board what had been said and started to believe that I was disgusting and that nobody liked me. As a result of that I tried always to please people. I tried to fit in by doing what I thought others wanted me to do, by being what I thought others wanted me to be. I tried to make people happy and do whatever I could to please people. What I didn't realise was that because of that I was growing and developing and nurturing a huge self-loathing and a huge fear of failure and rejection. I was growing and developing an idea that I was not okay and that I had to be something other than what I was in order to be okay.

I began to always feel that I was not good enough, that I would not be good enough. I compared myself to other people and always felt I would not be able to reach the standard I believed other people met. So by the time I was going into secondary school I did not believe in myself and did not believe that I would amount to anything or that anybody could like me. So I began to act that way. I started to believe the lies people had spoken over me and the labels people put on me. That began to affect me negatively. *Failure, useless, stupid, ugly, disgusting, smelly, not as clever as... no good, not as good as your sister, clingy, odd, strange, friendless, ect...* And as I began to compare myself with other people it seemed I could never match up to them. Even in the church I looked at others and thought they were so much better than I, felt that I would never be as holy as they were, that I would never be that close with God. I looked at the way everyone else worshipped and concluded that I could never do it like that.

It was that belief system that made it very difficult for anyone to get close to me or to like me because I expected them to hate me, and I made it very clear that I expected that. I lived that. I even constantly asked people who clearly cared for me if they hated me, because I could not understand the fact that they cared for me. I became a not very nice person. I lied to be the person I thought others wanted me to be. I grew in anger and constantly waited for the next moment I had done something wrong. Thus people did begin to dislike me and reject me, and because I was so difficult to be around and to be friends with, I would constantly snap at those who did stay with me and blame them for the pain I felt. I pushed people away by putting my feelings on them and expecting them to hate me. I made myself friendless, the thing that I had been told I was. It was a self-fulfilling prophecy.

Words are so powerful, and the way we receive words is important as well. I spent so long believing the lies, the lies that said I was a rubbish person. It wasn't until I started to believe the truth about what God says about me that I started to live in the identity God has for me. That's why it is so important to know what God is saying about us— and the way to do that is to get into God's Word. When we read the Bible, it really refreshes us and encourages us. It is important not to believe the lies other people speak over you but rather to receive the words God speaks about you. We should ask that *who am I?* question slightly differently. Instead of asking *who am I?* we should be asking *what does God say about who I am and who does God say I am?*

If we believe the labels of the world, we are believing lies and lies come from satan. If we believe we are just a sinner or just a failure, we just end up living our lives expecting at some point that we will fail and mess up. We end up being trapped in that feeling of failure. We must begin to try to see ourselves as God sees us—as saints who are good even though we sometimes mess up and make mistakes. When we start to believe what God says about us, we will raise our sights of who we are and what we can do. We will eventually end up expecting to live our lives as God made us to live and how He empowered us to live.

We curse ourselves, we curse others, or let others curse us. All those years that I said day after day "I am ugly" over myself I was cursing myself. I used to look in the mirror and say it to myself or tell a friend, "I am stupid." I believed I would fail at everything I did, and so I would declare that. In the spiritual realm I was allowing satan to have a foothold in me. I was speaking death and decay over myself. I was allowing that belief and lie about who I was to become a reality simply by speaking it over myself. The more I said it aloud, the more I believed it, and then it took root and satan got into my thoughts and brought decay to my life. If I declared I would fail, I would not allow myself to achieve ... and thus I would fail.

The Bible tells us that "the tongue has the power of life and death" (Proverbs 18:21) this means that what we say has power and effects the spiritual realms. In Genesis we read that God spoke the world into being. When Christ died on the cross He had suffered silently until right before He died. With His dying breath He declared "It is finished" (John 19:30). Our words speak out and satan must flee at the name and truth of Jesus. Do not let your words bring you any more death. In your words you have the power to curse or the power to bring life.

God will not let you go; with Him you are truly secure. God never let me go. He was always there. I did not always see Him because my pain seemed to take over everything. When the anger and bitterness got so bad, it was I who gave up on looking for God in those times, but God never left me and He will never leave you. I went on a journey to realise that God was not far away and never moves. I was far away; I had moved. As soon as I accepted that God was there, that His steadfast presence in my life was the rescuer from my pain not the cause of my pain, then I realised that God would not just give up on me one day even when I made mistakes. I had been waiting for myself to mess up really badly and hear God say, "That's enough now", and give up.

Yet He didn't. Even when we mess up really badly, God is not far from us and He will not leave us. Even if you read this book today and really believe what it says and choose to declare life into your life but then go and declare negative things in the morning and begin to feel those negative things again, God will not let you go. God will not move. Even in times of trouble and hardship, financial difficulties, relationship problems, pain and suffering, God will never let you go (Deuteronomy 30:8). The questions are: Will you forget to look for Him? Will you find it too hard to look for Him? Will you turn away from Him? Even though it might appear that you cannot see God and do not know where He is in your situation, I can guarantee you that He is there because it says it in His Word. He will not let you go, and because I know Him and I know He loves and doesn't abandon those He loves.

If you are having a difficult time or carrying great pain, God will be there when you suffer. He is in the midst of all our difficulties. Look for Him, cry out to Him, and turn to Him. He will make Himself known, even if only through a tiny whisper. I know that it is hard for those who have suffered great loss and great trials to accept that God was there in trials. As I look back on my life and see times when I have struggled and suffered and felt pain, times when I did not and could not see God at the time, I now see that He was evident, and so present, in that situation. Because of that, I have begun to try to look for Him and turn to Him even before I can see Him. It surprises me how often I find Him and see

Him in the midst of my pain just by believing the truth of who He is and by speaking truth over myself and accepting that He did not create my pain.

Jesus wept for my pain. Jesus wept for your pain. It is so important to know Him. I understand that the church often expects us to trust God before we even know Him, which leaves us wondering who He is. We cannot trust a God we do not know just because somebody else says He is good. My biggest problem was that I could not bring myself to trust God. I could not trust His Word, and I could not entrust myself to Him, and yet as a Christian attending church I knew I was supposed to because I was expected to trust God. I knew that if He was to be the answer to my healing I had to trust Him. It wasn't that I didn't believe in Him. I knew Him and had met Him at various times throughout my life. I had felt Him and had seen Him.

I did not particularly blame God for anything, and it wasn't that I didn't understand the Word. It was simply that I did not trust Him. Having talked with many people today who have been believers for many years, I have found that this feeling of not being able to trust God or His Word is not at all uncommon. When I was younger, I could not find any book or other resources that even talked about the struggle it can be to trust God. So I felt like I was the only one who could not trust Him, like I was the only one struggling. I thought everyone else could trust Him without reservation. I wondered what was wrong with me. Now I know that there was nothing wrong with me. When I realised there was nothing wrong with me because I didn't trust God, I found it easier to deal with. Until then I hadn't been able to deal with my lack of trust in God because it carried so much shame and guilt and condemnation. I felt so unclean and wrong because I couldn't find anyone who would talk about it or any books to read about it.

I tried to talk to my youth leader about it once, but she was young and could not seem to understand why I would not or could not trust God. Her only answer was that I needed to "have faith." The problem was, I thought I did have faith. I believed in God and prayed, went to church, and did all the right things. It wasn't that I didn't believe in God. So I got more and more confused until I could not even understand what faith actually meant.

If faith meant *trust*, then I began to wonder if I was actually a Christian. Then I questioned how I could have faith in a God I didn't know. How could I trust a God I did not know? I knew Him to be real because I had met Him and felt Him ... and yet somehow I did not *know* Him and had no relationship with Him. If you just met somebody for the first time or somebody was only an acquaintance, you would not share your soul intimately with him or her. You would not immediately trust and believe in everything the person said. Without relationship you cannot be expected to trust. We do not expect people to trust us completely the moment we meet them. So why then do we so often expect it to be different with God?

Just because we believe in God does not mean that we have an intimate—a close, open, and trusting— relationship with Him. I realised then that it wasn't a matter of suddenly deciding I must start trusting God and then somehow wake up one day trusting Him. I could not trust God until I knew Him. Thus I realised that the key was getting to know God. Of course we don't have to trust God with human standards, but we are human in a fallen world. God is okay with spending time getting to know us; God is okay with us wanting to encounter Him more and more as we grown in our relationship with Him.

Trust is only a part of what it means to have faith. Yes, I have faith in God. We often talk about having faith in what He says or that He will provide, which in essence means to trust. But it is impossible to trust that somebody you do not know will provide or to trust in the things he or she says. Getting to know

God is like getting to know anybody. We must spend time with Him. We must listen to Him, talk to Him, find out about Him. The more we do that, the more our trust in Him will grow. Only then can we expect Him to heal our pains. Only then can we hand Him our intimate innermost thoughts.

So often in pastoral care settings I have heard the words "Trust me, I'm a Christian" or, worse, "You can trust me because God asked me to care for you." These statements and others like them can actually be abusive and can actually cause far more damage than good. Think about it. Just because you believe in God or believe that God whom you trust says you are equipped to care does not automatically give you the right to have somebody else's trust. Trust is earned in relationship with another. The problem with these statements is that they are controlling and give the other person nowhere to go. They only bring condemnation and guilt because when the person whom you barely know cannot trust you, they are made to feel as though they *should* be able to and thus when they don't they feel guilty.

These statements lure people into opening up to you before they are ready or want to in a very unsafe way. Please do not make statements like this, and if anyone ever says these things to you know that it is okay to say, "No, I don't trust you". You are not expected to trust anybody or even God without knowing them. Of course there are many wonderful Christian people who are trustworthy and whom God may have put in your path to help, but until you know that and know God for yourself because they have earned your trust, you are not expected to trust them.

Do you know God? I knew of Him for so long and had even encountered Him time and time again, but yet I lived a half-life. I was walking around dead inside but calling myself a Christian, yet I did not know God. I did not understand that believing and doing all the right things in church and calling myself a Christian was not living in the wondrous authority of my freedom. Being a Christian was so much bigger than I had ever imagined! So many Christians do not live in the full authority of the life they could have.

I pray for you today that you will encounter God in a way you never have before, that He will find you right where you are. Whether you know each other well or are only just beginning to know of Him, I pray that you will have such a deep love encounter with Him that you will never be the same again. I pray you can get to know Him and His beauty so that you will be able to trust Him and His word.

CHAPTER SIX

WHO IS GOD?

I am now a far cry from that awkward, shy teenager in that photograph of my performing arts college group. Even looking at the photo brings back memories that almost make me sick as I remember the self-loathing, bitter confusion, and depression that seemed constantly to drape over me like a wet black shawl that I could not seem to shrug off my shoulders, no matter where I went or how much I tried. The longer it was there, the more tightly it clung to me and the more I took comfort in the presence of my wounds. I would drape myself in my wounds because they were something I knew, they were something I could understand.

I grew to be attracted the emotional pains that I carried around, a heavy load that got progressively heavier and more burdensome to carry as the months and years rolled by. I became worn and jaded as I began to feel comfortable in the known—my sorrow—and frightened of the unknown—possible healing. The known was fast becoming the pain, the sorrow, and the raw self-hatred that was ever growing inside of me. I had no creative outlet for my pain. I had no way of understanding the pain I felt. I felt that I had nobody I could talk to even though there were many loving people who cared for me in my life. My family watched heartbroken as the happy confident child I had been slipped away into a sea of broken, hurting anger, but I didn't know how to express what I felt.

I didn't know how to talk about my pain with anyone such as the members of my family who cared for me because I didn't know what was causing the pain. I felt so alone in a vast sea of brokenness—a brokenness I couldn't even explain, a hurting deep within me with no apparent cause. I just knew that I could never find safety amidst the fear and insecurity I felt. It was obvious to all around me that I was in pain, but it was not a pain anyone—least of all *I*— could understand. I had not been able to talk with anyone about it and in fact there didn't seem to be anything to talk about. I didn't know how to talk about it, and I didn't know how to express my emotions. That left me trapped, as though I was in a cage and desperately longing for freedom even though freedom seemed scary and so far removed from what I knew. Yet now my life is so full of wonderful colours. What was once just black is full of so much colour and excitement.

I find myself smiling when I am least expecting it. I look in the mirror and I can see the beautiful, free and happy woman God made me to be. I no longer carry my wounds around like a comfort. I am layer after layer shrugging that black shawl of depression off from me. Underneath I am finding more and more layers of a wonderful, compassionate, loving, happy content young woman. I am secure in who I was made to be and I am each day loving the adventure of life that Jesus is taking me on. However, it was a choice. I didn't get to this point alone, it was a choice to decide to shrug off that black shawl of depression and dare to see what is underneath. I am free from that blackness. Freedom is a choice.

Once you choose to be free, the first choice in coming to a place of freedom is getting to know God. I mean, to really know God, to know who He truly is, what He stands for, and how He defines us. Then we can choose to trust Him for our healing. Until we know God and know Him intimately as the good and loving and caring Father that He is, knowing Him for who His character is, we cannot rest and trust in Him and His Word. We must allow

God's voice to tell us who we are and to define us. God longs to know you intimately. God is love; He cannot be anything but love. God can only create good. God loves you, His creation, so dearly, but until you can be assured of that you can never fully trust God or His Word. I could not trust God just because He is God. I had to be able to trust Him because I knew Him and knew who He is and found Him to be trustworthy for myself.

That set me on a journey to search deep into the Bible and to question God to help me come to a place of being at peace in who I am and who I am made to be. I am so excited to live my life in the place of freedom I am now. I look in the mirror and declare that I am beautiful and believe it. I laugh and smile and have so many wonderful friends. I am doing things and finding myself more and more caring for others who are hurting and broken. Over the last few months I have stopped and suddenly realised more and more that I am the healed, supporting one in so many relationships. That did not come to me over night; it was a long, hard, and deliberate journey. I had to fight built-in thought patterns and wrestle with everything the world was telling me was true. I had to choose to question everything, not just take it as fact. I had to dare to believe the complete opposite of what I had always believed. I had to take time and energy to build a relationship with God as my loving creator. I had to learn to trust Him and His Word.

So who is God? Well I can only share with you some of the revelations that I found in my own journey. It is your choice to decide to believe or not. Your personal faith walk is solely between you and God. It is up to you how you engage with Him. In the next several pages I will share some of what I have found to be true of God and His character. I challenge you to look deep into the words of the Bible to find out who God is. I challenge you to seek Him. Talk to Him and listen for His reply. I cannot tell you what to believe or what to think. It is your choice to trust, your choice to accept or disbelieve. I cannot put God, our marvellous and wondrous creator, in a neat definition that fits in a book. I have only a few pages to describe who He is, and all the books ever written would not be enough to say who He is. I pray and hope you will pray with me that as you go on to read just some of the revelations of who God is He will meet you in your reading. I pray His Spirit will fill you, and I pray through Him that you can begin to choose life or continue to choose life over death through Him and in meeting with Him a little deeper.

We hear and are often told that God is the *Great I*

Am, but who is that? No matter how you have seen God or what you think of God, the truth of who He is is written in His word. It is in the Bible that we see God deeply. As with any friend, we can only start to get to know God as we spend more time with Him and talk to Him and wait to see if He will reply. In the listening we can know Him.

Remember, when you meet somebody, you cannot ignore them and not talk to them for a week and expect to know them closely. You don't talk at them and not wait for them to reply. You don't read about them like a personal profile or read their CV but never meet them in person and then expect to know them intimately and trust them implicitly. Of course you don't! You have to meet them first, spend time with them, see them, get to know them, and see their heart. You watch what they do and see how they treat you and others. So why do we not do that with God?

Let me share with you a little of the revelation I have had of who God is. Know that I pray that He will meet you and reveal Himself to you through these words.

Firstly I came to see that God is good. That is an absolute fact. Our **God is good**. Our God only does good. Our God only makes good. All good things come from God. "Taste and see that The Lord is Good" (Psalm 34:8). As I have said earlier, there is pain in the world. satan is of the world, and he is the creator of pain and suffering. We are in the world, but as followers of Christ, we are not of the world (John 17:16). Even though we are not immune to the darkness of the world, the world is hostile, and we can feel that fire. All of us have at some point in our lives experienced pain. All of us have had to face some form of rejection or hardship. We have all had our struggles and have felt suffering. As I mentioned earlier many of us then struggle to understand how God could have caused that to happen to them or their loved ones.

The truth is: He didn't. God is good. He cannot create your pain. If you are in any way feeling that He did then you immediately stop your healing because God cannot heal you of the pain you are blaming Him for. The question of why God allowed suffering to happen (even if He did not create it) is big, but we must first recognise the goodness of God and understand and believe that He is not anything but good. While there is evil and sin and pain in the world, that pain saddens God. Jesus weeps for our pain. While God will make all things work for good (Romans 8:28), God did not make our pain or want our pain.

satan surrounds us with many lies about God and His character in the world. It is very easy to become sucked into believing those lies until to the point that we really don't know who God is anymore. It is very important for us to stay firmly rooted in God. While all pain and suffering come from satan, it is important to recognise the beautiful things that come from God. Love, grace, friendliness, blessings, peace, joy, and laughter all come from God. As do tears, which are a God-given response to our pain and are in themselves healing and beautiful. I have come to know how beautiful good and Godly things are. I have come to understand how turning to God in my pain helps because He is good and He restores.

The next characteristic of God that helps us to trust and understand Him is the truth that **God is our Father** who has called us His children. The Bible says we are all children of God (Galatians 3:26). We are not just children tolerated from a distance but we can in fact call God "Abba," which means Daddy. We can call God our Father "Daddy." For many people their experience of father here on earth is far from perfect because they are sometimes abusive or just completely absent. Some people feel abandoned, let down, hurt, violated, uncared for, or misunderstood by the man they call father or the man called father who was never there. We are being called the fatherless generation, but we are not fatherless. That label does not need to be declared over us because we have a Father in God.

Some like me have a good loving dad around who is part of their life. My Dad is a dad who cares, loves me, worked hard to look after me and his family, watched me grow, prayed for me, and has been there for me. Yet still he is only human. He is not perfect and cannot be perfect.

Though I love my Dad and look up to him, I still struggled to call God "Father". The beautiful thing is that I can now call God my Father because I have come to understand that I do not need to judge God with human standards because God is good and only good. He is a good Father. God is my perfect Father, and I know His love and acceptance are absolute and perfect. There is no love like God's love.

Whatever our experience of our earthly father was, we are all children of God and God is the perfect loving parent who knows absolutely what is best for His children, not in a mean, strict kind of way but in a loving gentle daddy-like kind of way. The Father characteristics that God has are perfect. His fatherly protection, provision, warmth, tenderness, kindness, and gentleness are all perfect and complete. In the Bible God has revealed Himself to us as all these things. Before God we can be little children wide-eyed and excited. No part of God's fatherly personality is absent, abusive, or unloving. While some of us wrestle with the idea of punishment or discipline from a father, it is important to remember that discipline in itself is not wrong and in fact comes from the same root as the word "disciple". Discipline is God's loving way of "discipling" us to enjoy the free and whole life in Christ He intends for us. Some people in my own life have loved me with a constant yet firmly strict approach to ministering to me, creating healthy boundaries of right and wrong for my own protection and growth. God's discipline is like that, loving in its approach. It is not angry or intended to cause pain nor is it just to punish us to satisfy Him. Remember that God is good and everything He does is good. Discipline is not punishment.

"It is impossible for God to lie" (Hebrews 6:18). **God tells the truth.** "God is faithful" (1 Corinthians 1:9). **God is faithful** means that everything God promises He is going to do, He *will* do! God has proven Himself faithful and true many times. Anyone who seeks God will find Him. Faith is a gift, and it must be opened. God cannot do anything that is not of Him, so God cannot lie and does not lie. To be faithful means to be true and trustworthy and to fulfill promises. There are countless examples in the Bible and in people's testimony that indicate that God has kept all His promises, even years after He made them.

God does not always keep His promises instantly (in other words, on our timetable) or in the way we expect or imagine. But He *will* keep His promises. In a world where we are constantly let down and short-changed, I found this truth of God to be a great comfort. In a world where what is advertised or promised is not always what is delivered or comes to pass, it is comforting to know that we do not have to worry about whether we can trust what God says and promises or not. We can be assured of His faithfulness because God will never leave us or lie to us because He is forever faithful.

Maybe you are like I was, so riddled with guilt and condemnation. Maybe you feel you have done something so bad that you are living with the heavy weight of that great shame. Maybe you feel that you could never be forgiven. Maybe you cannot forgive yourself. If so, take heart! "The Lord is full of compassion and mercy" (James 5:11). You need to hear this: **God is merciful.** And because He is merciful He will forgive *all* your sins. It is in God's nature to have mercy. It is in God's nature to forgive. It is we who pile the condemnation on ourselves because of our sin—not God. God does not condemn; He forgives. It is we who cannot forgive ourselves, and so we think God cannot forgive us.

Many people have asked me why God shows us mercy. The answer is that God compassionately cares about us so much that He wants to show us His mercy. Isaiah says, "The Lord comforts His people and will have compassion on His afflicted ones" (Isaiah 49:13). This means that God cares about you He cares about what you are going through, about your struggles and your pains, about what you need, and about what makes you sad. God cares so much about you. God has so much compassion for you even in all your pain.

Just take a second to look at the life of Jesus. Look at how He was moved with compassion for the broken people around Him. Look at how Jesus served others to help in practical ways. Jesus was moved with compassion for anyone who was sick, suffering, broken, hurting, and in need. Look how He responded to the blind man, Bartimaeus (Mark 10:46-52), or the 10 lepers (Luke 17:11-19), or the young boy afflicted by demons (Mark 9:14-29). Look how Jesus responded even when He was hung on the cross: "Father, forgive them, for they do not know what they are doing" (Luke 23:34). Jesus reached out His hands and loved everyone. He set captives free. He embraced mankind with compassion. See how He talked to the woman caught in adultery (John 8:1-11). Did He ridicule her? Did He condemn her? Did He reproach her as many would have and many were about to? No, He spoke compassionately to her and forgave her. That is exactly how God feels when He looks at you. God looks at you, knowing everything you have done, and is filled with compassion for you. God has mercy on you. God forgives you. Nothing is too bad for God's grace and mercy. It is such a wonderful feeling to know that God has such deep mercy for us.

We human beings change all the time. Our friends and family are not the same as they were a few years ago. I know I am not the same as I was at 16, not just in outward appearance but in virtually every other way. I am not the same as I was even last month or last week. Though some changes are for the better, maybe some are not good at all. Whichever, the fact is, we change. We can rest assured, however, in the fact that **God never changes.** It's simply impossible for God to change. James 1:17 says, "Every good and perfect gift is from above, coming down from the Father of the heavenly lights, who does not change like shifting shadows."

Once we are sure of who God is and that He is good, we can be at peace that He never changes. What causes us humans to change has no effect on God; we change all the time due to circumstances and challenges we have to face. We might change our beliefs or values based on what influences us, but God never compromises or changes His values. We might become weaker or stronger in any given situation through our constant learning and prior experiences, but God never gets weaker or stronger because He is all-powerful. He does not learn because He is all-knowing. Outside influence— such as the influence of evil and sin—does not change God. God is always bigger than sin and stronger then satan. God is always the same, unchanging, and because of that His purpose for you and your life is unchanging. This gives you eternal significance.

We read in Psalm 33:11: "the plans of the Lord stand firm forever, the purposes of his heart through all generations." This shows clearly that God's plan never changes. God's plan was formed at creation and is still the same today. And you are a part of God's plan. Ephesians 2:10 declares: "we are God's handiwork, created in Christ Jesus to do good works, which God prepared in advance for us to do." What God said all those years ago in the Bible is still the same today because God never changes and therefore His Word never changes. God never planned bad things to happen to you, but He does renew and redeem all the bad things that happened for His good. God restores.

These are but a few attributes that describe who God is, His character and His heart for you. God longs for you to turn to Him and to spend time with Him. We can get to know Him by reading more about Him and from Him in the Bible, also by talking to good Godly people we trust about Him. We can spend time with Him by giving Him space in our lives to speak and meet us where we need Him to meet us. He is there waiting with so much beauty and goodness. His Spirit wants to fill you. He wants to give you a true revelation of His character as you meet Him. It is such a personal thing. He is crying out to let you get to know Him deeper and deeper. Choose to meet Him, choose to let go of all the pain and mess you are clinging to because it feels "safe", and let God who is love meet you and fill your heart.

CHAPTER SEVEN

NO TIME FOR REGRETS

A friend recently told me about a woman she had read about in the newspaper who lied for the purpose of getting affection and attention. The woman had told those dearest to her that she was terminally ill when she was not. My friend took little time in expressing her obvious disgust for the woman's actions. I found myself feeling a large knot beginning to build in my stomach and then for some unknown reason I began to fervently defend the woman from the newspaper article. I was quick to point out the woman may not have known that she was lying, the human mind is very powerful, and so she may have believed what she was saying. Or maybe she had started out knowing it was a lie but she had lied so long that it had become a reality for her. Maybe she was just too broken and hurting to really mean anything by it.

There is always a reason why people do things. My

heart pounded and my defenses flew at my friend's judgment against the woman and her actions without knowing the situation. I was quick to point out the story was from the point of view of those she had lied to, not her own. The people she lied to would be hurt, and hurting people are quick to cast blame. I implored my friend to consider other options, other possible reasons behind the woman's actions. I challenged my friend to consider that even if the woman had lied knowingly and intentionally for some kind of attention, that in it's self shows the woman to be clearly confused or broken in some way.

Then my friend spat a question making her disgust clear, and in that moment I realised something I had not realised before. My friend spat in disgust, "That's awful! It's sick. How sick do you have to be to do something like that?"

I stopped and I felt the knot in my stomach tighten, "very sick," I replied numbly. I knew my friend meant "sick" in a disgusting kind of way, but I meant sick in a broken, ill, hurting kind of way. I knew the woman in the newspaper article was sick, mentally ill in some way. Anyone who lies in such magnitude has to be sick because I don't think a person in their right mind could tell such lies.

We have all done things we are not proud of, things we would much rather pretend we had not done. I often look at my life and feel like I want to regret, but a few years ago I promised myself that I had no time for regrets, not because there are not things I wish I had never done but because I have come to know one thing: I cannot change my past, but I have a future and by making good and Godly choices I can change my future. I do not want the mistakes I made in my past to continue to shape my future into something best left alone. Imagine being like David and having all your mistakes laid bare in a book— God's Word, no less— for all eternity. None of us would want that! I am not about to share with you all of my mistakes in this book, but I will share with you one of my biggest mistakes and one I never want to repeat. When I say I don't regret it, I am not saying I would do it again. I am saying I have come to a place of acceptance. I accept the mistake I made and I know it to be wrong. I will not deny what I did but nor will I let it shape who I am going to be in the future. I am who I am now, and that is not governed by my actions some years ago. I have come to understand that there is always a reason why somebody is acting the way they are, a reason behind the things they are doing. Although it doesn't excuse it, it may well explain it and help with how we deal with things after they have been done.

Have you ever told a lie? Have you ever made a choice to say the wrong thing? I don't believe anyone can honestly say they have never lied. I have lied—big lies. You see, some years ago in my brokenness and pain, I, like the woman in that newspaper article, told many people close to me that I was terminally ill. I am not going to try to justify that or make it anything other than what it was: I lied. I will say, I was hurting, I was confused and I did not understand the concept of love, not really. I didn't understand that the people I was telling this lie to loved me. I didn't understand how they would feel to know that somebody they knew was terminally ill. It wasn't that I didn't care; it was that I didn't understand. I think partly I didn't want to have to think about a future I could barely see. In a strange way I believed what I said. I felt so angry and sad for who I was then and for what I did. Yet I had to choose to let it go. I had to stop blaming myself and cutting myself up for the choices I made then.

For the years following I have hid from this truth, ashamed and not wanting anyone to know what I had done or, who I used to be. I've often talked with people about the effects and consequences of that sin, how I hurt people, lost good friends, had to leave my church of 21 years. I gave up on my dreams, I left the Bible College where I was studying because of how broken I was. Over the years I've admitted I hurt people, that I was wrong and even that I lied. But I have hid in shame from what that lie was for too long. Yet the truth of it is that I have no time to regret because Jesus loves me so much. In His eyes my sin is no worse than anybody else's sin and He remembers my sin no more.

It has been a beautiful exchange—Jesus took that lie and any other sin in the world and died to rescue us from them. I was hurting and I was lost and Jesus, our loving redeemer reached out and saved me.

A tiny part of me knew I was lying and that it was wrong, and I hated myself for it. But the rest of me, the bigger part of me, acted without reason, without shame or guilt. The bigger part of me was trying to survive. I didn't want to focus on living. I don't know why, and I don't even remember now the first time I lied. All I know is that in a strange way I have come to understand what I did because I recognise I did it because for some crazy reason it was the only way I could survive. For too long I lived a half-life. I was waiting to die and somehow that was easier to cope with because I saw no future. I didn't set out to hurt anyone; I didn't set out to be selfish or manipulative. I just set out to survive in a way I knew how. Sadly, though, I did hurt many people and I could not find it in myself to forgive myself for the lies. What I said was wrong, and I rarely want to admit that I have done that. I lost most of the friends I had at the time. They were good and Godly people and though I never see them I still think of them from time to time.

I am not telling you this because I want to look good in some way or want sympathy. I am telling you this because I think it is important to face our sin. Sin is a horrible word, a word that often evokes the thought of the word "judgment". Yet grace is a very beautiful word, but a word very rarely explained. To look at grace we need to look at sin. Sin is anything that is not of God—thoughts and actions that are not what God would want for our lives. God is not a hateful God. He does not command law nor punish us for our wrongdoing. He loves us and forgives us unconditionally. As I said in an earlier chapter, however, there are consequences to every action. Every time I told that lie about being ill, I hurt God, and ultimately I hurt everyone I told it to, I hurt my family and their relationships with their friends suffered. Truthfully it also led to my being hurt and my world being torn apart.

Every time I told somebody I was terminally ill (or any other lie), I found myself moving farther and farther from God. Sin separates us from God, not because He leaves us, not because He turns His back on us, but because *we* turn our back on Him. When I was lying in the way that I did to many people I rejected God. God does not give a commandment *do not lie* because He is waiting for us to slip up so He can punish us. God has a commandment *do not lie* (and all the other commandments) because He knew it was wrong. He knew it would hurt everyone, the person lying and the people who were lied to, and Him. God knew it would please satan and bring victory to him because lies are from satan. The wages for sin is death; death is separation from God.

Ultimately my sinning the way I did brought death—death to my relationship with Him and with others. It brought death to me because it killed me inside and guilt and shame entrapped me. That's what sin does because sin is death.

When God was doing His work in me by changing and shaping me in His refining ministry, I found my hardened heart softening to His way of doing things. Many wrote me off as a hopelessly selfish liar, too far gone to be reached. I was branded selfish and saw anger and pain in the eyes of those who had once cared for me. I couldn't stand to think I had caused such pain to the people who had cared for me. I couldn't stand to face what I had done. It destroyed me, and I began to see myself as hopeless. I saw no future, no way out. That led to there being no hope

115

in my mind. Many people I knew were turning their backs on me, not because they didn't care but because they couldn't be the ones to help. It was complex and it was something people did not really understand. "You need help," they said, "but I can't help you". I heard that over and over again. I wondered if anyone could help me? Could anyone help a broken young woman who had sinned? I had hurt so many people and let them down, and I became someone whom I couldn't even face.

I remember looking in the mirror and despising what I saw looking back at me. Every time I tried to pray all I heard was the angry, hurt words of those I had hurt. I didn't know how to look at God and not see anger. Many would say I ran away. I ran, all right. I ran straight into the arms of the God I knew as a child. That didn't look how I thought it would look, though. It meant having to leave the church I had called home for 21 years. It meant joining a church my parents were attending, where I knew very few people. It meant facing the reality of what I had done in ways many would not know about. It meant seeing a doctor and agreeing to receive mental health care. It meant accountability and accepting that for that time in my life many of the dreams and aspirations I had for my life were lost. It meant stripping right back down to the empty shell of who

I was and giving myself up to God. It meant allowing myself to be broken—real Christian brokenness.

Those I had hurt called for my repentance in the way they wanted. They expected I would work to pay back the time, energy, and love they had given me and insisted I do what they thought God asked of me, including twisting Bible passages to make it sound as though I had to work for grace. It meant being used as a scapegoat for other people's lies, mistakes, and relationship breakdown, and I went in search of freedom where there was hope not blame. I walked away. I lost everything, but out of that I have gained far more than I had ever imagined. I have a full and vibrant relationship with my Lord Jesus. I have freedom beyond anything I ever dreamed of, and I have amazing friends who have walked an amazing journey with me for my freedom. The church I joined where my parents were became like a beautiful home full of wonderful friendships and people who said, "You need help, and in God I will do my best to help."

I went on a path, which meant I set out to fight for true, ultimate freedom in Christ for myself and for anyone else I would meet in the future, not just to repay the hurt and the damage I had caused. I found healing, freedom, and wholeness, and in a sad way that meant walking away from those I had hurt. Of course that does not mean that I was right to hurt them, but there was nothing I could do that could ever make it right. I could never fix the damage I caused. I cannot change my past, I could never repay what I had done. Yet I do not have to, Jesus paid for what I had done so now I can change my future, that is the wonder of grace.

As part of that journey to freedom, I did seek out the chance to be able to say I was sorry to those I had lied to and hurt. I wrote a small note of apology to each, and in doing so I took responsibility for my actions. That was not simply a "sorry I got found out" apology, but a heartfelt, sincere expression of sorrow, and nobody can argue with a changed heart, a changed life. I did not change on my own. I could not change on my own. I changed because of a filling of Holy Spirit, because new loving people came alongside me and said I was worth caring for and ministering to and because Jesus gave me His grace. Through that He restored what I had lost. I have a church to belong to and call home. I have good and Godly friendships, and in wondrous awe I am back studying theology at a new college full of amazing and beautiful staff and students.

The grace of the Lord is a wonderful thing! Jesus came to Earth because He loves us, but He came for so much more than simply to forgive our sins—He came to restore all that was broken. Yes, Jesus forgave our sins. But I think what that actually means is so much more than the forgiveness of our sins. Jesus died to restore us to a greater relationship with God. Jesus died to tear the curtain of the temple. Whereas before only the high priest could enter the dwelling place of God, now, because of what Jesus has done, we can all approach the throne of God with bravery and confidence, as it says in Hebrews 4:6. The moment we accept Jesus as the Son of God who died to save us, we receive the absolution of our sins.

I think it is important for me to try to explain forgiveness and the absolution of sins. In our western culture often when we talk about Jesus' forgiving our sins we are talking about Jesus' absolving us of our sin. The two are very different things. Yes, Jesus *forgave* us, but on the cross He also *absolved* us.

Forgiveness and unforgiveness are about blame. The definition of forgiveness is to choose to not blame. That is different from saying "it was okay"; it is different from saying, "it doesn't matter", which is another way of saying "it has no consequence". And forgiveness is not saying, "I forget". We have all been hurt by somebody else in our life. People who have bullied me have hurt me; if I forgive them I choose to say I no longer blame them. It does not make what they did to me okay; I am not saying it wasn't wrong because it was wrong. I am not saying that there are no consequences because of it, nor am I saying that I will forget. All I am saying is that when I forgive I no longer carry blame towards those people for their actions. That is in itself a hard choice—but it is a choice.

Sometimes I have to make that choice for that same hurt daily, hourly, and that's okay. The more I have made that choice in my life, the easier it has become. That is because all the anger, rage, bitterness, resentment, fear, shame, and guilt attached to sin is from satan, *not* God, and it is unforgiveness that harbours those thoughts. Anger and bitterness cause death inside. If you are harbouring resentment or bitterness towards somebody for the things they have done against you, it is you who is suffering because that bitterness is eating away at you and causing you even more pain. If you do not put down the blame, then you will carry that blame for another and that will lead to bitterness growing deep inside of you. You will become hardened, and that blame, that unforgiveness, will eat away at you. Most likely that person who has hurt you is off living his or her life, unaware of hurting you or possibly not caring about hurting you, getting on with life. Meanwhile, you are the one who is continuing to suffer for the other person's sin; you are the one who is continuing to carry the pain. Forgiveness is not saying it was okay. Forgiveness is not weak. In fact, it is a brave thing and is saying, "what you did to me was wrong, but I choose not to blame you anymore". It does not mean that you then forget and become a doormat and let it happen again. Sometimes forgiveness does look like continuing a relationship or friendship, but other times forgiveness is saying, "I don't blame you any longer, but we cannot have a relationship now because of what has happened". That is okay. There are people who have hurt me in my life who I have forgiven and yet I have made a choice to no longer see them. Forgiveness is about making a choice to let go of the anger, let go of the bitterness, and let go of the blame, and through that you find freedom.

Atonement and the absolution of our sin comes only from Jesus Christ on the cross. Through the atonement sacrifice in Jewish law the people could be forgiven of their sins. The high priest would perform the atonement sacrifice to cleanse and absolve the people of their sin. When Jesus came, He became the last high priest, and in doing so He became the atonement sacrifice for our sins. This means that through Jesus we can be absolved of our sin. Absolution is wiping the slate clean, blotting out our wrongdoing, taking the consequence of our sin, and alongside forgiveness — no more blame— it means we are completely free of our sin through Jesus.

The consequence of our sin is death—a spiritual death here on Earth, a separation from God while we are here on Earth not just with regards to our eternity after death. If I live a malicious selfish life and constantly hurt people, I am constantly going to feel the effect, which is the consequence of that sin. This is why it is important to try not to sin. It is not just about eternity—so it's not as if we can simply do whatever we want now and then Jesus forgives us and after death we go to Heaven. Sin destroys us; it literally kills us inside. We live in a painful mess, a pit of despair and mourning. That's what is amazing about God's grace—grace screams love right into all our guilt and shame.

CHAPTER EIGHT

THE GIFT OF GRACE

The root causes of our issues and dysfunctions in life are always the same no matter what situation we are in or what circumstances we have been though. Too often the world's way of healing is to try to heal the dysfunctional way of living. However that is like putting a bandage on an infected wound without dealing with the infection. The problem with that is that it only deals with the issue on the surface, for a time. By doing that, the issue always comes back, either in a bigger, angrier wound or in some other dysfunctional way of being. The biggest problem with that is that so often guilt is attached when the person's dysfunctional way of living seems to never stop.

In my own life, I could not stop being angry or seeing myself in a bad light. I began struggling with my food and began self-harming because I was trying to stop being angry and rude all the time. Yet because the root causes in my life were still there those dysfunctions grew. If I didn't deal with my feelings of being stupid, I was never going to stop trying to cope with those feelings. At that time in my brokenness the only way I felt I could cope was to not admit what I felt about myself. That lead to me having a distorted idea about food and about myself.

If you are trying to help somebody who is showing coping through self-harm, the worst thing to do is say, "Your coping mechanism is wrong and you need to stop it," and then give him or her no other way of coping. For example, if somebody is surviving by self-harming it is very damaging to tell that person to stop self-harming because it is wrong—even though it is—because the person cannot simply stop because they have been given no other way of coping. Worse yet, now guilt has been heaped on them for doing something wrong. I understand how heart-breaking it is to see your loved ones hurting themselves in such a way. You want to help someone who is hurting, but please never tell them to stop a dysfunctional coping mechanism or, even worse, ask them to promise you they won't do it again, and then give no other outlet for their pain or no other way of coping. If you are somebody who is trying to cope in such a way please seek help. Don't stay silent. Do not feel guilty if you cannot stop straight away. Alow Jesus to minister into your hurt and the very roots of your pain.

Your pain has a voice that has the right to be heard. Let the pain have it's voice, let the pain have it's dysfunction, voice out the anguish that you feel. Let God work in the pain and in the voice of the dysfunction. Then and only then can a person stop harming themselves or stop bursting out in fits of anger and other dysfunctional ways of coping.

Our pains are always rooted in things such as fear, shame, guilt, rejection, bitterness, and blame. These come from satan and are not what God wanted for us. They can come to us through any circumstance or situation we go through. Before I could deal with the lies I was telling or the dysfunctional choices I was making in my life I had to face and heal the things I had been through in my life. I had felt like my life was one disaster after another, one struggle after a another that was never ending. I had to to change something in my life. Before I could do that, however, I had to accept and deal with the feelings of blame. I had to give voice to my anger. I had to wrestle with who God was, and who He had been in my life. I had to learn to see myself as God sees me. Through that I learnt a new way of being, a new way of building relationships. It took time and a lot of angry rages and tear-filled ministry sessions. Over time I stopped blaming others for my darkness. I stopped being rude and aggressive. I stopped acting out to those in authority and stopped pushing away those who were closest to me. I began to understand the care and love of God. I accepted that others wanted to help, and I softened my hard, rebellious, and angry heart to admit I had done wrong and that I was hurting. I opened up and let friends and family in to my world and my pain, I dared to admit there was something not quite right in my life, and I was prepared to seek God to find out what that was.

The first thing I had to do in all of that was to *choose* to want to forgive.

Forgiveness is a real sticking point for many people. People often find it so hard to forgive. The very idea of forgiveness annoys people and often just seems so wrong. In a *worldly* sense forgiveness is wrong. It shouldn't be. Forgiveness can feel like going against the natural order of things. It is a very natural feeling to want to see somebody suffer in the way we have been made to suffer. I remember last year talking with some friends from work on our lunch break. One had seen a programme on TV about a woman, a mother, who had made the extremely beautiful and brave choice to forgive the man found guilty of murdering her son. My work friends were saying this mother either could not have been in her right mind or didn't love her son.

That made me so sad. My friends at work just didn't see it. They didn't understand that the mother was not crazy but beautiful. She loved her son so much that she made a beautiful choice to forgive the man who had killed him. That woman is an inspiration. Yet my work friends scorned her and said she could not have been a good mum and that if it were their son who had been murdered they would not rest until that killer was dead. They even said they would kill him themselves and do the time in prison. That is so heartbreaking, but that's the culture we live in, a culture of revenge in which forgiveness means you are crazy. At the root of that is a lack of understanding of forgiveness.

I have seen Christian people wrestle with the verse, Ephesians 4:32, in which we are told to forgive as Jesus has forgiven us. I have heard people say they are a bad Christians because they cannot forgive as they have been forgiven. People say it's too hard, too big a thing, yet what they don't understand is that it is one of the only things that is going to help them.

Unforgiveness destroys everything but more importantly it destroys our relationship with God. It is not possible to carry unforgiveness in your heart, and have a good and healthy relationship with God. The two cannot go together. Unforgiveness towards others, ourselves or God damages our relationship with God. If we won't forgive then we can't receive forgiveness. Those of us who have been around the church any length of time will know we need to forgive. Many of us will say "I forgive" but it needs to be more than words. It needs to be a true love encounter with Jesus transforming our heart, thus deeply bringing us to a place of no more blame.

I think the problem is that often people think that forgiveness means forgetting and saying it— whatever the offense might have been—was okay. Forgiveness means neither of those things. It is not okay that the son of the woman in the TV show was murdered. It will never be okay and that woman will never forget her son or how he died but she can choose to no longer blame the man who killed him, not because she is saying he didn't do it or that she wants to be his friend now. No. She is saying she does not want to hold bitterness towards him anymore, that she doesn't want to hold anger because by doing so it is only going to destroy her life. She wants to remember her son in a good way not feel overwhelming bitterness and anger every time she thinks of him. That mother made the hard and difficult choice to no longer blame the man who killed her son. She may wrestle with that choice daily and have to make it again every morning, but she still makes it because she knows the beauty of freedom from the bitter root of anger and vengeance. Forgiveness frees her; it becomes a beautiful thing for her.

That woman was not absolving the man of his sin when she chose to forgive him. This shows the difference between forgiveness and absolution. The woman cannot absolve the man and is not expected to do that. Only Jesus can absolve sins. The absolution of sin removes guilt and takes the punishment of sin, which is death, which is separation from God both here on Earth and for eternity in Hell. We cannot remove the guilt of sin or take the punishment on behalf of others. Yet God loves us so much that He does not want to be separated from us, He does not want us to go to Hell, and so through the blood of Jesus on the cross our sins are forgiven—no more blame—and we are absolved of our sin. We have no more guilt and the punishment is taken from us.

In Jewish tradition God resides in a part of the temple called the Holy of Holies. The high priest would perform the atonement ritual with a sacrificial lamb for all the people. Wearing his priestly religious garments, once a year he would go behind the curtain into the Holy of Holies to offer the sacrificial lamb before God for the atonement, which is forgiveness and absolution, of the people's sin. This was the only way sin could be forgiven.

Jesus was the last high priest. He exchanged His garment of righteousness for our sinners' rags. He became the sacrificial lamb, and this means we now here on Earth have the authority to walk with God in that intimate relationship He intended. The curtain in the temple was torn as Jesus died, and now through Him we, too, can enter the Holy of Holies and stand before God as priests. The Kingdom of God is here on Earth now for every believer. The kingdom of God is not just heaven after we die. The kingdom of God is where God is and God is in every believer. In the kingdom of God there is no pain, no sickness, no guilt, there is nothing that is not of God. Therefore this is who we are in Jesus. Through Him we have the authority to overcome all those things which are from satan. There are only two powers, God or satan, nothing in between. If it is not of God it is from satan. Yet through the death and resurrection of Jesus we have the authority to stand firm against satan. We have the authority to stand in Jesus and in His name tell sickness to go, to tell pain to go, to tell anxiety it has no place in us. I am not saying we will never be sick, in pain or anxious again but I am saying that when those attacks come we can stand and we can fight with the true authority of Jesus. satan is always wanting to rob us of the life Jesus intended for us. satan will do this with power and in any deceptive way he can, satan is the ruler and prince of lies. Yet we can stand as holy and righteous priestly saints.

Jesus did that for me, for you, for the man who killed that woman's son, and for every person who has ever lived or who will ever live. That's the wonderful thing, the beautiful gift should we choose to take it. I have accepted Jesus as my Lord and Saviour and in doing so I accepted the gift of grace, that is the gift of forgiveness and absolution of my sin. If you have accepted Jesus as your Lord and Saviour you, too, have been given the gift of grace. You, too, have been forgiven and absolved of your sin through the blood of Jesus as He died on the cross.

What is so wonderful about grace and so special is not that we *will* have it but that we *do* have it. We have grace here and now. Jesus has died for us to have grace if we will only reach out and take it. There is no price to pay, no cost for Jesus to give us His grace. It is a free gift. Grace is not dependent on our works. Grace is that beautiful forgiveness that says there is no more blame and absolution that says there is no more cost. It is hard to believe, and often we put guilt or shame on ourselves or others in our hurt and anger, and yet the God who created us says no more guilt, no more shame. Maybe we look at society and the blame culture that is fast getting worse and worse and simply cannot seem to reason where grace fits in this world.

That was my biggest issue with grace. I had come to understand what it meant, but yet I had not been able to accept that such a beautiful thing had a place in a world so desperate to blame and judge. It took me a long time to understand that we are in the world but not of the world because we are of Jesus, that God sees things differently. God sees things His way. If we have wronged somebody and they choses not to forgive us, our freedom and eternity do not depend on that. Our future, our freedom, our eternity *is* dependent on the grace of God. God gives His grace to anyone and everyone, but it is up to each and every one of us to receive it.

This is why we think we cannot forgive as we have been forgiven, because we confuse forgiveness with atonement. We can choose to not blame but we can't atone. We can't take the consequences of sin, only Jesus can, but he doesn't expect us to. To forgive as we have been forgiven we need to understand forgiveness.

CHAPTER NINE

CHOOSING TO FORGIVE

Since that day in the children's tent when I was 6-years old I knew Jesus as my Lord and Saviour, but I didn't really know what it meant that He was my Saviour. I didn't know grace. I remember talking with a woman in my church who cared for me when I was in my late teens. Sitting at her house late one night I tried to tell her how Jesus had not died and rose for my sins. I could accept Jesus. I didn't deny Jesus. I had seen Him and His nail scars, but I was so trapped in my shame and guilt that I could not see that Jesus could forgive me because I could not forgive myself for all the things I thought I had done wrong. That woman's response, which I didn't understand at the time, was to ask "What makes you so special?"

I thought she didn't understand what I was trying to say—that I wasn't special. That was the point. Yet now I understand what she was saying, I had just told her: "Jesus, the Son of God came to Earth and died for everybody's sin and rose again to defeat death and give everybody eternity in Heaven if they accept it. He did it for everybody in the whole world, that is, except for me." Now that seems so ridiculous but it didn't then, but her question makes sense now, what made me so special? I know there may be people reading this book who are thinking just as I was, so I ask you now: What makes *you* so special?

I don't say that to condemn you but only to make you realise that Jesus died and rose for everyone's sin so that we could have freedom and eternity, even you, even that murderer or that child abuser you read about in the newspaper. That is tough and hard to accept, but Jesus sees us all as equal and our sin is all equal. The wages of all sin is death, which is separation from God. While the consequences in the spiritual realm are the same for each sin, the consequences in the physical realm are different. If I lie to you to hide something from you I won't go to prison for it, but your trust in me would be damaged. If I murder somebody, however, I will go to prison. That person would have lost their life and their friends and family lost a loved one. The consequences for the two in the physical realm are very different because one is seen as a much *bigger* sin.

Yet for God in the spiritual realm, the consequence of both sins is death, which is separation from God. Jesus died and rose for both sins so that a deep and intimate relationship could be restored and maintained here on Earth because through Jesus the Kingdom of Heaven is now, when God looks at us He does not see our sin—He sees us transformed to be like Jesus. This also means we can live for eternity with Him. This can be extremely freeing *if we look at it right*. This is not condemning. I know that for some being told your sin is the same as a murderer's is shocking and condemning, but please do not see it that way. Instead of focusing on the sin side of the equation—what *you* did, focus on the salvation side of the equation—what *Jesus* did! It is freeing because God frees all people from all sin—from murder to taking a pen home from work which is stealing, to making judgments of others and bitterness and unforgiveness, which in themselves are sin.

We may never know whether somebody we have wronged chooses to forgive us. I no longer see some of the people I have wronged in my life. I will probably never know if they have forgiven me or not. That decision is theirs and theirs alone, and if I wait for them to choose to forgive me or tell me they have made this choice before I can feel released from my shame and guilt, I will live a life of bitterness, guilt, shame, and self-condemnation and will spiral down into self-loathing with all the dysfunction that comes along with that. Your life is for now and for living! Embrace the fact that God has forgiven you and restored you so that you can walk with Him in freedom. So many people find themselves trapped in a life they are not happy with when a beautiful life in freedom can be theirs. For so long I have carried the heavy burden of self-condemnation. Guilt and shame has been a constant presence and for so long it nearly destroyed me. Don't let it destroy you, it does not have to because of Jesus.

Forgiveness is the first tool and the first step to living the free life Christ died for you to have. Forgiveness is a choice. Yes it's a very hard choice and easier said than done but it is possible. Different people tackle it differently but I am just going to share with you a few of the things that have helped me on my road to forgiveness. It's a hard thing to actually forgive, that takes time, the first step is to choose to *want* to forgive. That may sound crazy but unless you want to forgive then it's going to be too hard to do that actual forgiving. It is about choosing to want to say I don't blame those who have hurt me anymore, not because it's going to set them free but because it's going to set you free. Forgiveness isn't for the other person, it's for you.

Choosing to forgive is hard but very freeing. If you really feel like you can't but you are at a place where you want to lay down the bitterness and lay down the anger and choose to no longer blame then it's important to ask Jesus to help you to forgive, if you feel like you want to forgive but you can't yet then ask Jesus to be there and ask Him to help you forgive, this is a really special thing. Wanting to forgive, wanting to lay down all the pain, all the resentment and stop blaming the other person or yourself can be a huge step. It's a big thing, but it is possible because all things are possible through Christ.

Don't let satan rob you of your future by convincing you that Jesus doesn't forgive you or that you can't forgive yourself or that you can't forgive others. You can, I know just because you choose to want to forgive doesn't mean that you have but without wanting to you wont be able to. It's not a choice to say "it was ok and it doesn't matter" it's a choice to say "I don't blame you anymore, I'm fed up of this anger towards you", the anger you carry is only destroying yourself.

The next step is to declare it, I had to stand with a trusted person who was supporting me and say out loud with my own voice who I was forgiving and what for. Some people I had to forgive for many things, some of it quite big things, others I had to forgive for tiny little things, yet each were just as valid and each needed forgiving because each held pain and anger. Once I had done that I said out loud that I was forgiving that person. It didn't fix everything instantly, it just meant that I was declaring into the spiritual realm that I was no longer blaming them. It took time for my feelings and even my thoughts to catch up, that was up to God to deal with. It's sometimes a constant choice to say "I forgive. I don't blame" sometimes daily, second by second as I thought the thing I needed to forgive. The more we say it both outwardly and inwardly Jesus works through us. Remember Jesus restores all things. Restoration might not always look the way you want it to. Forgiveness is not the easy option, but it's the healing option. I know how hard choosing to forgive can be.

Accepting is the first step. I spent a long time trying to ignore the hurts I felt. Yet hurts never go away, not until we accept them, stop ignoring them, and bring Jesus into them. It's important to take the time with Jesus and with another person who you trust to think through, and talk about all that has hurt you. It's important to bring Jesus into those bad memories. Trying to pretend you haven't been hurt never works.

Take the time to be honest about the pains you've faced. Don't try to face every pain at once, let each pain or regret surface, each one at a time. It's taken me years and years of determination, commitment and stumbling along to get me to where I am today. It takes time to let the healing continue in you, but over time it gets easier. Let the pains out, let the reality of how you feel be expressed. You can do this in a good and healthy way by asking Jesus to be with you, and making sure your safely with somebody you trust.

Ask Jesus to show you the things you need to forgive. Jesus is gentle and loving. Let His gentle ministry hold you and guide you. Everything has a season, even healing. I have come to find out more and more recently that healing often comes in layers, not all at once. Jesus will show you what is right to deal with at what time.

Invite Jesus into those memories or regrets. It is important to bring them into the light by sharing them with somebody you trust. This is confession, there is something spiritually powerful in sharing your pains, your regrets and your shame with another person. This way they are not hidden. satan moves in the darkness, God moves in the light. When you share the things that satan distorts to trap you, he looses his grip.

Ask Jesus to show you where He was when the painful things happened, or when you made those mistakes. Allow Jesus to show you His love in your difficult memories. Allow Jesus to show you His grace, and mercy on your regrets. Jesus was there, He was always there, and He is with you now. Jesus was there when I faced the painful things. He wept with me in my pain. He was there and knew the guilt and shame of my bad choices. Jesus hung naked and humiliated on a cross, in agony for the darkness and sin of the world. Jesus Himself said at the time of His death "it is finished" (John 19:30). He meant utterly and completely. Sin is over, the price for our debt paid with His death. Don't let yourself be held by the bondage of anger and bitterness, or guilt and shame. Those things are so destructive to us and to our lives.

For a long time I was held captive by anger. It was an anger that would come bubbling up in me, like a rage I couldn't control. I would lash out, and snap horrible things at the people who loved me, and cared for me the most. What I didn't understand was how destructive it was to me, and to others. I pushed so many people away with my anger. I hurt many people and kept people at arms length. People didn't always think I was a nice person to be around and I was a slave to that anger, the root of which was unforgiveness which I was carrying around and not even realising I was.

If there's things you know you've done wrong you can talk to Jesus and ask Him to forgive you, you can tell Him you're sorry. Repentance is about saying sorry, and trying to not do it again. It's about standing with a pure heart, and saying to Jesus "help me to not do this again." Nobody is perfect, it is rare a person who is trapped in a cycle of sin, can say sorry and then just stop that sin straight away. It is a journey and a process we are all on, let God guide and lead you along the way. Let forgiveness into your heart.

There are three types of forgiveness, forgiving others, forgiving yourself and forgiving God. Usually if a person is good at forgiving others they are not so good at forgiving themselves, and if they are good at forgiving themselves they are not so good at forgiving others. Of course there is always exceptions to the rules. It is forgiving God that gets the most people annoyed, either because people don't agree it is or should be needed, or because they find it too hard to do. I am just going to look at those three aspects of forgiveness now:

Forgiving God.

People struggle with forgiving God because they

think it implies that God has done wrong, but it doesn't. Deciding to forgive God is about *you* not God. God cannot do wrong. God is perfect and good. But if forgiveness is about choosing to not blame, then forgiving God is making a choice to say, "I no longer blame God". It is a hard thing to tackle and wrestle with, because if we know God is a good sovereign then we know that in reality He cannot be blamed for all the wrong things that happen to us, or the evil things in the world.

Yet the single issue that cuts to the very core of it is that we then say, "Okay, so if God is good and sovereign and has the authority and ability to stop evil from satan, then why doesn't He save us from it?" The beautiful point is that He has.

God did not make us to be puppets. He didn't make us purely with strings to be controlled by Him. He made us to have free will, which is an extremely special and beautiful thing. He wants us to use that free will to do the right thing, to make choices, the right choices. Sadly sometimes we all make wrong choices or disaster happens and we find ourselves blaming God. God is not to blame for the things that go wrong in our lives or in the world—satan is.

The more we blame God, the more we don't trust Him, which is exactly what satan wants because then

God cannot heal us. I do not have an answer for why bad things happen in the world other than satan is evil and creates evil and spreads evil. satan wants us to live in pain and bondage. In that bondage, in that guilt and shame, there is only One who can save us. Only Jesus can bring us out of the darkness we find ourselves trapped in. Let's not look at the sadness of the pain, let's look at the goodness of the rescue. So often people blame God for the things that seem to go wrong but don't want to thank Him for what goes well.

We so often ask, why God doesn't save us from evil. Why He doesn't take our pain. Yet He has. God saved us the day He sent His son to die on a cross for us, and it was for our freedom that Jesus came. If you want to walk in that freedom, live in that life that Jesus died for you to have, then you have to choose to forgive God, you have to choose to stop blaming God for your struggles and your difficulties even when it feels as though He hasn't done anything for us or does not care. I have found in my life that when I am angry at God, when I am blaming Him for all that has gone wrong in my life, I cannot then trust Him or expect Him to help me or save me.

I cannot say I have ever really, deep down, blamed God for all the things that went wrong or the confusions I have faced, but I did often wonder why He didn't save me. It wasn't until I understood and accepted that when I choose to stop blaming Him, I can choose to accept Him and His healing that He gave me the day He died on the cross to rise again in glory over all things of satan. When we carry bitterness, resentment or blame towards God for what we think God should have done, or what He didn't do or what we think He did to make Him responsible for our pain, we fail to allow Him to heal us and restore us.

Forgive God, let go of the blame, and choose to accept how much He cares for you—so much that He has set you free and given you the tools to live in His authority, beauty, and freedom.

Here is a prayer you could say if you want to choose to forgive God:

God, Thank you for you love. Thank you that you are good. I am sorry that I have blamed you for _____ , I renounce that blame. I choose to forgive you and stop blaming you for this. I know you are not responsible for _____. Amen.

Forgiving Yourself

This is something I have wrestled with for too long. I grew to hate what I had done and the wrong things

I hoped nobody would ever see. I let my sin fester into guilt and condemnation. I let it grow and stagnate inside of me. Carrying sin around is like carrying death—a rotten decay of the spirit. I felt I carried a terrible stench everywhere I went that I could never seem to brush off. I had come to know Jesus had forgiven me and I believed it, really believed it deep in my heart, but I could not seem to be able to accept that forgiveness for myself. I carried the guilt and the shame, and somehow guilt and shame made sense in my mind. I could not seem to stop hating myself for what I knew I had done. I knew that there were other people who had not forgiven me, and I think some part of me was ashamed of who I had become. I didn't like the wrong things I had done to people and was desperate not to do it again, but in trying to change so much I ended up destroying myself and my future, which seemed reasonable at the time.

I could never take back what I had done. I could never reasonably repay all the hurt I had caused people. I just felt hopeless and empty inside. I was so ashamed of the lies I had told. It wasn't until I learnt that actually not forgiving myself was destroying a future that could otherwise be bright and full of life and hope, that I began to find healing and freedom. I had to decide to accept what I had done, which also included admitting it. Even years afterwards, admitting to myself and facing up to the things I had done even in my own mind was hard, and it was then I realised how much of a grasp guilt and shame had on my life. I also had to admit my sins to God and honestly stand before Him and repent. I had to go to those I had hurt and where appropriate express my sorrow and apologise (though sometimes that is not appropriate).

Years later I found myself trying to hide the lies I had told regarding the non-existent terminal illness, and others. I didn't want my new friends and relationships to know about it. I didn't want my sin laid bare for all to see, though I found that hiding it harbours guilt and shame and lets them take deep roots. Guilt and shame only breed fear because you are constantly worried and fearful of what others will see in you. When I made that hard choice to accept and admit what I had done in my past, I was able to tell those who were supporting me currently. By telling others we bring what is hidden into the light. It is not about telling everyone—broadcasting our sins—but rather bringing what is hidden into the light by telling the select one or two people we really trust. If the sin is hidden, guilt festers. If it is not hidden but shared in true Godly integrity, then there's nothing to be ashamed of, nothing to hide from, nothing we hope others will never find out.

Shame loses its grip when we disclose ourselves and what we have done with somebody we trust. Once shame is gone and we experience acceptance, we can make a choice to no longer blame ourselves, make a choice to forgive ourselves. This principle can be applied to any sin or guilt. It took me years of carrying guilt and shame for a sin I saw as huge when deep down there were reasons I acted in certain ways and said certain things. It need not take that long, for when we start to practice forgiveness we find immediately how much guilt and shame we are freed from because we see how the bitterness and anger bind us when we have unforgiveness towards others.

Here is a prayer you could say if you want to choose to forgive yourself:

Jesus, Thank you for loving me. Thank You for what You have done for me on the cross. I confess that I _____. It was wrong I am sorry. I choose to accept the freedom, grace and love You gave me on the cross. I ask you to come into the guilt and regret I feel and help me to restore. Thank You that You make all things new. I choose to forgive myself for _____. Amen.

Forgiving Others

This is not easy and we cannot pretend it is. It is against the natural order of what the world says. Often we feel like we want to be angry and bitter because we have a right to feel angry because we have been wronged. Often we long for the person who has offended us or upset us to be hurt in the same measure that we were hurt. "It serves them right", we think. We feel like it is our right to have what we call justice. We need to stop feeling that way because we are the only ones who suffer when we do.

Unforgiveness leads to bitterness and anger, and anger leads to hate. If we carry unforgiveness towards others we carry anger, which will only lead to hate and spiritual death. To say "I choose not to blame you anymore" is not weak. It is brave, very brave and very freeing. We don't even need to understand why the person did what he did. We just have to understand that it was wrong, that it hurt, and that we can get healing from our hurts through Jesus. We do not need to blame the person anymore. We give that blame to God and let the other person reconcile before God. Let God deal with the judgment. There is always a reason why people do what they do; hurting people hurt people. Let God heal and restore their brokenness and show them where they were wrong. Let God restore them, while you let God restore you.

When I hurt a number of people with my lies a few years back, I don't know why I did it. It was not a conscious choice to lie and hurt people, people who in my way I actually cared for and loved. Sadly, I didn't understand what it meant to be a friend. I was hurting and wanted to find a way out of the mess I felt in my head. I guess that was selfish, but it wasn't selfish in an "I'm going take everything I can from you" kind of way. It was selfish because I was so hurt inside that my dysfunctional behavior hurt others, and I didn't realize how wrong I was until it was too late. Though we never know what is going on behind somebody's behavior, we are too quick to judge. Let God do the judging because when He looks at the person who hurt us He sees Jesus on the cross, just as He sees Jesus on the cross when He looks at us and our sin. As believers we are in Christ, that means we are being reformed and reshaped to be more Christ like – more forgiving.

Free yourself from the blame and the resentment because carrying such thoughts and baggage around is only destroying you. That person you are thinking about and getting all angry and bitter about is out living life, perhaps not even aware they hurt you. So let it be. Let God work in them to change and refine

149

them at the right time. You can make a choice to free yourself from bitterness, so choose not to blame anymore. Let God change and refine you.

It is not possible to forgive without the help of Jesus. It is because of Jesus' grace that we have first been forgiven. It is because Jesus has a heart of forgiveness that in Him we are forgiven and so able to forgive others. Don't expect that in forgiveness everything will be perfect. Forgiveness takes time. Jesus changes our heart to be more like His. Every time thoughts of blame, anger and regret enter your head it's a choice. It's a choice to say "*I forgive*" and deep down in your heart allow Jesus to shape you and change you. If that choice has to be made several times an hour, keep making it. Don't let the negative thoughts destroy you. Don't wait for feelings. If you wait to feel like you want to forgive it will never come. Decide it's time to let Jesus heal you. Decide that you don't want to carry the pain of anger and hate. It's time to pray for those who have hurt you. Pray for them and bless them. I'm not saying that's an easy choice to do that. There are many people in my life I could hate and blame and rage about, but I choose to pray for them and bless them. Not because of what they have done or because they deserve it, but because of what Jesus has done, and because He asks me to. Then and only then have I been able to know the forgiveness and blessing of God's grace into my life. Blessing somebody we would rather hate brings such freedom to not only us but them aswell. Pray for those who have hurt you.

Here is a prayer that you can choose to say if you are ready to forgive others;

Jesus, I thank You for Your grace. I thank You that You died for everyone and I thank You that You brought us out of darkness. I ask You now to be with me as I choose to forgive _____ for hurting me by _____ . I pray for _____ now and ask you to be with him/her and to bless him/her. I choose not to blame _____ any more. I ask that you help me as I forgive. Please come into this situation now and restore me. Please bring your healing touch and help me in my pain. Amen.

CHAPTER TEN

SALVATION'S FRUIT

The moment you accepted Jesus as your Lord and Saviour a wonderful divine exchange happened. Not only did you receive God's grace through the death and resurrection of Jesus but you also received His Spirit to come and live inside of you. God is in three persons—Father, Son, and Holy Spirit. They are three distinct persons of God each of whom we can grow in deeper relationship with individually, and yet they are eternally inseparable. They are in complete unity with each other. They are one God. Holy Spirit is the part of God who comes and lives inside of us. He is the part of God who comforts us, guides us, and fills us. When we talk about *feeling* God, we are talking about feeling the Spirit.

After Jesus was resurrected He said He would ascend into Heaven soon but would send One to comfort and counsel us (John 16:7). The One He sent is Holy Spirit. What's so beautiful about Holy Spirit is that He was there before all of creation. He has been moving among us since the dawn of time. He is that still small whisper that guides us or that loud voice that convicts us. Holy Spirit is the power of God and the seal of our salvation. This means when we were saved Holy Spirit came to live inside of us sealing our salvation (Ephesians 1:13). He is a life-giver and has great compassion for our brokenness. We receive Holy Spirit into our lives the moment of salvation, yet the ministry to us and through us and the filling of Holy Spirit is an ongoing process in our lives. The acts and works of the Spirit are called signs and wonders. The more we engage with Holy Spirit in our lives, the more we get to know Him, and through His presence in us and through us we can live in a deeper freedom and peace. It is the power of Holy Spirit in us that brings freedom.

We are all spiritual beings made up of body, soul, and spirit. Our body is all that you see and touch, all the outward parts of us as well as our bones and organs. Our soul is also called our heart, which is our mind, our will, and our emotions. Our soul is what makes us the way we are; it is our personality. Our soul is our inner identity. Our spirit is something very special. It is what makes us spiritual beings. Our spirit is what connects us with the spirit realm. The spirit realms are Heaven and hell. Our spirit can connect with the demonic realm or with the Heavenly realm. The Spirit of God is in the Heavenly realm. All that is of God is in the Heavenly realm. Only things that are of God are there. When we accept Jesus Christ, we accept the Spirit of God to live inside of us by aligning Him with our spirit. The Spirit of God changes us and transforms us to be more like Him. This means our spirit connects with the Heavenlies. Once He is living inside of you, He will never leave you, never turn His back on you. He fills you, He loves you, and He guides you. The Bible says that our salvation is sealed and there for all eternity. Your name is written in the Lamb's Book of Life, from which your name can never be removed or crossed out (Revelation 3:5).

It was the power of Holy Spirit who raised Christ from the grave, and now that power is living in you. If you let Him He will completely transform your life to be more like Him. He will set you free of any bondage of satan because where the Spirit of the Lord is there is freedom (2 Corinthians 3:17). True freedom in the power of the Spirit is a beautiful thing. It is not about giving up control and becoming a puppet; it is about you *allowing* God to do His wonderful work in you. Holy Spirit is a gentleman. He will not invade you unless you invite

Him in to fill you. There is a difference between His living inside of you as a saved believer and His moving within you. Many people are saved and thus living with Holy Spirit inside of them, sealing their salvation. Yet they are not transformed in Him but still move in their old ways. They are not born again, not aware of their authority over satan and his ways in their lives, and so they are constantly letting satan win and darkness consume them. Although Holy Spirit is rooted deep inside of us satan still moves, and there is light and dark in all of us and there will be until we go to Heaven because of corruption.

Therefore we have to guard ourselves against the enemy. Just as our spirit can connect with God's Holy Spirit, so our spirit can also connect with the demonic realm. Because of Holy Spirit within us satan has no claim to or authority over our lives, our bodies, or our minds. Satan tricks us and wants us to not use the power within us to stop him. We give him the authority by believing his lies or yielding to his temptation to sin we do not live in the freedom from such authority. satan is so very good at tricking us, at lying to us and convincing us that his ways are better and that we are trapped forever broken and hurting. That's where the choice comes in either to believe satan's lies or to believe the truth—God's truth. The best choice is to choose life, spiritual life which is a complete wholeness in our lives through the truth of Jesus Christ.

When Holy Spirit is living inside a person He equips them for the fight against satan. If you are a follower of Christ, Holy Spirit has given you the tools to stand in authority against satan and his lies. Holy Spirit is in your life to change and transform you. Holy Spirit is there to help you be more like Jesus. God Has chosen you and set you free from your old way. God equips those He chooses, and thus He helps you who He had chosen to become all that you can be and all that He created you to be. He does not expect you to be a certain way or to reach an unreachable goal.

There is not a *supposed to* as a Christian. You are not a failure if you don't feel you reach what you think is what you are supposed to be. God only expects and wants you to be who you are and where you are at and then in that place to open to Him and let His Spirit move in you and change you. God will equip you to do the rest. The more you read the Bible and get to know His Word, and the more you pray and talk to God, the more you get to know Him, which will empower you to be free from the things that trap you and hurt you. satan is trying to rob your relationship with God, but the deeper you go in your relationship with God, the more satan loses the battle. God has equipped you through His Spirit working within you and transforming you.

Holy Spirit aligns your spirit with His nature and transforms you and takes you from your old nature. In Galatians 5:19-21, the Apostle Paul tells us the acts of a sinful nature, meaning a nature that is not of God or in other words our old nature. He says, "The acts of the flesh are obvious: sexual immorality, impurity and debauchery; idolatry and witchcraft; hatred, discord, jealousy, fits of rage, selfish ambition, dissensions, factions and envy; drunkenness, orgies, and the like. I warn you, as I did before, that those who live like this will not inherit the kingdom of God." It can be very easy at this point to feel condemned and feel like a failure or begin to start judging others. That's not what this is about because as believers we are all in grace, and every single one of us will find things in that list that we know we have done in the past or even do now. The Kingdom of God is here now because of what Jesus did on the cross. The Apostle Paul is not just talking about Heaven after we die, he is saying that if we engage with those things on Earth we will live in brokenness and not live free. What is so wonderful, however, is that we believers don't live like that. There are times when we slip up and let our flesh, our ungodly nature, win. At times I am jealous, speak out in fits of rage or am selfish or any of those things. Any of them could tempt me. We all sin as long as we are in this corrupt, fallen world. That list describes part of any of us.

Yet with Holy Spirit inside of us, we are in the nature of God—and that nature is good. We are in Christ. We are secure in who we are and accepted in Him. God's nature is good and bears good fruit in our life. The fruit of the Spirit in your life is love, joy, peace, perseverance, kindness, goodness, faithfulness, gentleness, and self-control (Galatians 5:22-23). This fruit is not nine separate fruits from which we can choose some and not others, and God does not give some of us the fruit and not others. This is one fruit made up of nine different parts. We have each part in equal number. We often refer to the fruit as Spirit, and thus we hear people say "the Spirit of joy" or "the Spirit of self-control". This is just another way of referring to the fruit of the Spirit, so it is one Holy Spirit with nine attributes which bare beautiful fruit in our lives. The fruit of the Spirit is not things that you need to aspire to be or to have. These are things God has given you and equipped you with as His Spirit is in you. The fruit is the evidence of God's Spirit within you. It is the fruit of the Spirit that equips you on your journey towards freedom and helps you and changes you to

159

be more Godlike. The fruit of the Spirit is within us as a result of the presence of Holy Spirit in our life as believers, not as a result of anything we have done.

The nine attributes are as follows:

Love

God is love. He cannot be anything but love. He loves you so much that He sent Jesus, His only Son, to die for you. God has given you His love in giving you Himself in His Holy Spirit. The fruit of love is not for you to aspire to be more loving. Yes, God has called us to be more like Him, which means loving, but you cannot love until you have first been loved and know the love of God. It is the special gift of God's love in you that will transform you and shape you to be more and more loving towards others.

In 1 Corinthians 3:4-8 we read what the attributes of love are that: "Love is patient, love is kind. It does not envy, it does not boast, it is not proud. It does not dishonour others, it is not self-seeking, it is not easily angered, it keeps no record of wrongs. Love does not delight in evil but rejoices with the truth. It always protects, always trusts, always hopes, always perseveres. Love never fails."

God is love, and so this is a description of God. Holy Spirit is changing us to be more Godlike. In

His nature we will be more and more like this description. This is not something we need to work at and aspire to be and if we don't it means we have failed, no it's not like that. God has given us His love and because He loves us we will see and learn of love, and through that overflow of God's love for us we will be loving towards others.

Joy

This is a wonderful thing. God has given us joy! This is not a matter of "I must be happy all the time." Rather it is an inner joy, a rejoicing over who God is and what He has done for us. We may go through some extremely difficult worldly situations and see no reason to feel joy. That's okay. That's natural. We are not immune to the hostilities of the world just because we follow Jesus, but Jesus *has* overcome the world, it is satan who is in the world. This means we can carry an inner joy through which we can face adversity. In that joy we can say *God is good*. The things we go through may not be good, but in everything God is good. Let Holy Spirit help and guide you into saying and knowing that God is good. Through Holy Spirit in you, you will come to a joy that overflows. That's not a joy that says "everything is perfect" and puts on a fake smile. That's not saying "I'm fine, thanks" when you are dying inside. It is rather a joy that comes into you and through you with being shaped by Holy Spirit to say, "Despite my circumstances I am joyful because I rejoice in the Lord and who He is and what He has done for me."

Peace

Like joy, peace is a deep inner peace that comes from resting in God. This is a peace that comes into your heart by letting Holy Spirit shape and transform you. Often when we are hurting and struggling with anxiety and worry they become our constant companion. The Spirit of peace is the only thing that is really going to get deep into those worries and anxieties and calm them. You have no need to try to make yourself more peaceful because like all fruits of the Spirit, this peace is already in you. It's a peace that grows in you deeper and deeper as you grow deeper in a relationship with Holy Spirit. The more you get to know Holy Spirit, the more peace will fill you and still your heart. Anxiety must go because you have the Spirit of Peace. When you start to feel anxious, declare out loud with your voice that anxiety has no place in you. In Jesus Christ you have the Spirit of Peace, anxiety or worry are from satan and they must go at the name of Jesus through the power of the Spirit of Peace within you.

This isn't about peacekeeping, though through a

deep inner peace you will find yourself more peaceful in your relationships and in all that you do. Out of an overflow of the peace within you a deep peace will flow from you to others. You will respond to things more peacefully. You will not only be less anxious and less worried, but you will not strike out in reactive anger but find yourself in a much calmer position to respond. You will be at peace in your soul.

Perseverance

Perseverance is the fruit of God's Holy Spirit in you. Some translations read "patience," but that often leads to misunderstanding. Many people see this fruit and think it means they need to be more patient with people and not get annoyed, which too often means let people walk all over them. No! This is about God giving you His Holy Spirit through whom you can stand firm and persevere through the struggles and hard times. Because Holy Spirit is inside of you, you can withstand any hardship. You can push on and persevere towards the freedom He has given you.

Yes, we are also called to be patient with each other, which is part of being loving (as the fruit of love works in us patience will flow from us), but the fruit of perseverance is something entirely different.

When we face hard times, Holy Spirit will give us the strength and ability to persevere through them. As with all the fruit of the Spirit, as we grow deeper in Him the more His fruit will be seen in our lives. His fruit is already in us, so powerful and each of the nine attributes in equal measure. Yet it is us who does not see it. Just because you do not feel like you can stand through any hardship does not mean God's Spirit of Perseverance isn't in you. When we see somebody survive their struggles through God we know the Spirit of Perseverance is working through them. He can work through you to, that power to persevere filled you when you accepted Jesus. Again, this isn't something we need to aspire to be because by growing deeper in relationship with Him we will begin to see and understand that we have the perseverance to withstand any trial through Him.

Kindness

I used to be so angry, and that anger would come out in the way I acted. I often felt as though the world was against me and I had to defend myself against the world. That meant I wasn't always a very kind person. I am not sure where these thoughts came from, but along my journey as I have grown deeper and deeper in communion with Holy Spirit I have found myself being changed into His likeness. I have softened. My heart has become less selfish, and I am a kinder person to be around. I did have to choose to make choices to stop and think about what I do and say, but also like all fruit of the Spirit He shaped me and changed me to be softer and kinder, and it was not something I had to work at. His kindness filled me and I found myself wanting to be kind. As I faced the anger and the way I snapped at people I saw more and more His kindness in me.

Goodness

God is good. In Him, we are good. Through Jesus, we transform and change to become saints, God sees us because we are saints. God sees us and delights in us. In God's Holy Spirit we are made pure and good as we move with Holy Spirit to be shaped more and more like Him. The grace of the Lord is not something we work for. We do not have to be working to win our goodness and salvation. We are good in the eyes of God, when He created us, He looked at us with joy and said we were good. As a believer, you are not a sinner, you are a saint made perfect and good in Him and through Him.

So often in the church I hear the saying "I am a sinner saved by grace" No! We are not sinners, we are saints! Yes I know we sin, I know we make mistakes but that does not change who we are. Our identity is that we are saints. In Jesus God sees us and we are saints. Our identity is a sainthood and a priesthood. Stop trying to work for grace. You are good; you are a saint. You are saved. The Spirit of Goodness lives inside of you and is fully in you. Through Him you are good and in Him you never stop being good.

Faithfulness

The fruit of faithfulness in your life is that you are faithful to who God is and who you are in Him. The Spirit of faithfulness in you will help you to remain true to God and faithful to Him no matter what comes your way. Again this is not about your need to work really hard to remain faithful. The mustard seed is a very tiny seed, and the Bible says with faith that size you can move mountains (Matthew 17:20). I have seen it in my own life. Whenever I have had to face struggles that seem like huge mountains, I turn to the One who is in me, who raised Christ from the grave, and have a tiny bit of faith that He will overcome what I am struggling with. I have time and time again found that He does.

Keep your eyes fixed on Jesus, and in Him you will overcome. I know that is easier said than done, and there are times when I do not have faith in God's ability to help me overcome, but in Him and through Him our faith in Him is secure and will grow, He can do wonderful things. The Spirit of Faithfulness will help when doubt comes. Do not condemn yourself when doubt comes, doubt is real and it is a human response to hardship. Remember that tiny mustard seed of faith is all that is needed to overcome any mountain. When you look to Jesus you will see how little the problem really is in His sight.

Self-Control

The Spirit of Self-Control is in us. How amazing is that? I find this to be amazing. This is the part of the fruit that many people don't like. Many people see this as just sort of tagging on the end. Trust me when I say it's not like that. This is wondrous. So often satan sends temptation our way. Often we use the word self-control when referring to restraining from eating too much sugary food and cake. While that is true, it is so much more. Through the spirit of self-control within us we have the ability to resist any temptation.

The word self-control is misleading because this is not about control over our self or our self having control over temptations. Rather, it is about God giving us the ability to resist satan's temptations. That might be the temptation to lie or steal or overeat or be angry or blame God. God's Spirit working in us and through us gives us the ability to withstand temptation. When a temptation comes we can say, "I have the Spirit of Self-Control", and through God's Spirit working in us and through us shaping and transforming us we will be able to resist. This is because by declaring out loud with our voice that we have the Spirit of Self-Control we are telling satan that with God's Holy Spirit in us we can withstand temptation, and that he has no authority over the power of God's Holy Spirit. A Spiritual thing happens. satan must flee and those temptations become less and less. This is using the power of the Spirit of Self-Control. Never say you don't have Self-Control or that you don't have enough, because you do. The Spirit of Self-Control is in you and fills you. Again though, this is not something to work harder at or feel condemned for if you give in to temptation. That does not make you a failure. Be kind to yourself and let God's Spirit work in you, the evidence of that will be His fruit in your life.

The fruit of the Spirit is the characteristics of a Christian life. The more we connect with God and Holy Spirit, the more we move with Him. We will never be fully able to show the fruit of the Spirit. If we could we would be God, because we would be perfect, and we are not God. God does not expect us to bear the fruit of the Spirit completely and perfectly. He helps us to become more like Him. He gave us Holy Spirit through our salvation so we already have this fruit like a tree planted and growing that bears good fruit. In the struggles it is helpful to declare out loud with you mouth that you have the fruit of the Spirit. For example in anxiety declare "I have the Spirit of Peace." Or in doubt declare "I have the Spirit of Faithfulness." This is because as I said in an earlier chapter our words have power. Hearing it aloud can reaffirm it to us. Our heads are often full of so much confusion and voices from satan, speaking the truth of the presence of Holy Spirit out loud breaks into that confusion. Also satan knows the truth but is banking on the fact that you do not. By speaking it aloud satan hears you and so has to leave for you are taking back the authority. You can ask Holy Spirit to fill you more and more and lead you and guide you even more each day. Listen to Him and let Him lead you.

Here's a prayer you can pray to ask Holy Spirit to fill you even more:

Holy Spirit, thank You for Your work in my life. Thank You that You have sealed my salvation and that You are at work in me healing and restoring me to be more like You. I ask You to fill me and renew me again today and every day. Fill me with who You are, and with Your power in me help me to withstand trials and be more like You. Amen.

CHAPTER ELEVEN

IDENTITY

Having looked at who God is and the fruit of Him in our lives, let's now look at the image we hold of ourselves for a moment, or what we call our self-image. Think of that image and belief you hold of yourself. Think about the pains you have had to face and the things you've overcome to be sitting here today reading this book. Think of the joyful things you have been through and the things you have achieved. Think of who you are. When you look at yourself, who do you see? What is your self-image? By self-image I mean the description and belief we have of ourselves, and the evaluation we make of our whole being and identity, everything about us. It also includes the amount of acceptance and peace we have over those beliefs and descriptions we carry of ourselves. Self-image is absolutely everything we think and believe about ourselves—whether good or bad, our whole selves and our whole being not just our outward appearance. Imagine everything that you are, not just your outward appearance but everything that makes you who you are—what you think, how you act, your desires, hopes, dreams, your likes and dislikes, what you own, how you feel, absolutely everything. Then make an evaluation of what you see. How would you make that evaluation? What do you have to weigh it against, to decide if that which you see is good or bad? That's the real sticking point of this issue because how and what we use to make decisions and evaluations about ourselves is more important than the evaluations themselves.

Many voices play a part in that evaluation process. We use many standards to judge and define ourselves. Although we usually think we are using our standards to judge ourselves, more often than not a poor self-image is the result of using the wrong standards on which to base our feelings and beliefs. Where do we get those standards from? Who is influencing our standards? Who influences what we do? Who maintains our standards? Well, there are our peers, our family, our culture that bombards us with magazines and social media. Then there are the church standards and how we feel we should be to be a *good Christian*. There are our teachers, our bosses, our neighbours, our soaps and TV shows, and so many other outside influences in the world. All these things are making judgments on us and influencing our beliefs and judgments when we look at our whole selves. Though we often feel that some of these places and things expect us to live up to a certain standard, the pressure to do so actually comes not from them but from us. Because we are looking to so many different sources to define our self-image and our identity we find a dislike or a confusion in ourselves. We end up resenting the outside influences that "make us" who we are when the truth is, our self-image comes from inside us when we choose either to let those outside influences define us or to look to another, higher source for our self-image.

Our western culture is creating a generation of people so obsessed with their self-image that we are now basing our self-worth—who we believe we are and who we believe we should be—on all the wrong influences rather than on the truth of who we truly are based on who God says we are and who God says we should be. Our self-image shapes our identity, which is defined more and more by outside influences based on the world's lies rather than on God's truth. These worldly influences are so subtle that some people may not even realise they are shaping their identity and self-worth on lies.

Some people may feel that they are okay and happy with themselves and don't have a negative view of themselves. The real issue, however, is not so much what you think about yourself (even though many would have you believe it is). I want to ask you to look deeper and challenge yourself: If you think you are okay, how do you define "okay"? What does it mean when you say you are "okay"? On the other hand, if you are not really liking yourself, what are you using to define who you are? You see, I believe that it is not about whether you think you are okay or not. The issue is where we look for the truth about who we are and the source of our identity. What standards are we using to make judgments about ourselves, whether good or bad. The real issue behind the growing feeling of self-loathing in our culture arises from who or what we compare ourselves against to judge whether we are okay or not.

What we use to define ourselves can overtake us and become a pressure to be a certain thing and to act and be a certain way. We often end up feeling like we are waiting for a judgment, constantly being judged for the kind of person we are, usually by those we believe are better than us in some way or who have it all sorted and perfect, even though deep down we know that nobody is perfect. It becomes easy to lower ourselves and put everyone else on a pedestal—not because they are in any way better than us but because we are taught to constantly judge and define ourselves against unhealthy and unreachable goals. Daily we agonise and fear over this and worry about what people think of us and if we are good enough or not. Daily we want and long for that verdict to be that we are important and valuable, that we are okay, that we have somehow made it. That is when we begin to shape ourselves and force ourselves to be what we believe we *should* be.

So the question is: Where is that *should* coming from? Where are you looking to define the identity you feel you should be? Have you ever really stopped and thought about it? As Christians we know that God has made us and thus His voice is the one that we need to listen to. Yet more often than not God's voice is the last voice we listen to. God's voice gets drowned out in the loudness of our celebrity culture. Our TV advertising denies us the right to see beauty other than that which is in the airbrushed model. Social media paints our friends' lives to be like highlight reels—one beautiful experience after another win—because very few people put up their bad-hair-day photos or low exam grades on Facebook. Yet we use others' commentary and what they write on social media to define how we don't quite match up to them. Somehow we let the world's voice, the voice of lies, fill us and scream louder than the voice of truth, the voice of God. I therefore want to challenge you to consider God's voice, to think on the picture God gives us of ourselves? And what evaluation does He make of us? Where is our identity? How are we defining our identity? Do we listen to God's identity and His image of us, or do we let the world shape our image of ourselves?

For so long I let the world dictate to me who I should be, and yet I could never seem to fulfill what I thought that was. I could never reach the goal. I could never quite get there —never quite making it to where I longed to be, or who I longed to be. I could never quite get to where I thought I ought to be. I was never able to look in the mirror and like what I saw. For too long I had known the voice of lies and even felt as though I knew the voice that called me ugly. I felt I knew the voice that told me I was stupid. The voice that told me I would never be liked screamed so loudly, and I listened to it and let it take a deep root within me. The voice that told me I would never fit in with my peers seemed to overwhelm me. The voice that defined me as immature screamed, and I let it destroy me. The voice that told me people were nice to my face but hated me behind my back laid down its claim in my mind until I no longer heared the truth. God's voice was drowned out.

While I was listening to the many voices in the world—voices that came from satan to distort the truth— and allowing those voices to define who I was, I was not even trying to hear God's voice anymore. I wanted freedom. I wanted to look in the mirror and like what I saw. I wanted to be able to invite a friend out for a drink, and not fall into a terrible pit of self-hatred, as I wondered what part of me they were too ashamed to be with when they responded "no, sorry, I would love to, but I'm busy." I did not want to put my self-loathing on them in such an unfair way. Yet I could not find the freedom I desperately desired and hungered after until I turned to the One who had already come to set me free, the One whose voice I was allowing to drown out. We cannot find freedom in the decay of lies but only in the beauty of truth.

Self-image becomes about more than what we think because what we think can become a self-fulfilling prophecy, which happens when what we think becomes a reality. What we believe about ourselves determines how we act. If we believe good and Godly things about ourselves, we will act in such a way and carry ourselves well and with confidence and beauty. If we believe satan's lies about who we are, the lies of the world, then we will live out those lies in our behaviour. If I believe I am ugly, I will act that way—ashamed, shy and quiet, hiding away in social gatherings, feeling unworthy and comparing myself to others and never seeing myself as beautiful as they are. I will constantly assume others think I am ugly when they seem not to talk to me, and I will not consider the possibility that maybe they just picked up on my body language that says "don't talk to me." If I believe I am ugly, I will never allow myself to match up to what I feel it is to be beautiful.

This will then lead to my being unattractive to others because all they will see is an outward portrayal of what is inside. For so long that was me. I believed I was ugly and walked and lived my life as though I was ugly, always fearful of meeting new people, always fearful of being noticed, believing everybody must see me as ugly I as saw myself. Those distorted beliefs grew roots of dysfunction in my life. I stopped washing or brushing my hair for a long time because I saw no point in caring for myself because I thought I was so utterly ugly that no amount of effort I would put into my appearance would make me in any way beautiful. The problem was that my lack of self-care led to an unattractive, uncared-for appearance, which the world could have defined as ugly. My belief is what led me to not care for my appearance, and in turn that lack of care led me to look, feel, and be called *ugly*.

The important thing to notice is that it was the belief that came first and led to that being lived out. Yet even if I had cared for my appearance, if I believed my appearance was ugly then I would have presented myself in such a way that others would not be interested in getting to know me, which would only fuel the feeling of being ugly. So where did I get those feelings? In my case, I looked at what the world says is beautiful and *decided* that I was not that. I felt I did not and could not meet that standard. I did not look to the truth. If I had looked to the truth I would have known that God created me and God can only create good. Had I looked at the truth I would have known God called me beautiful. But I didn't. I chose instead to look to magazines and celebrities heavily covered in make-up, designer clothes, and photoshopped images to give me an inhuman idea of beauty.

So my question to you is: Do you live in the truths of the Bible or do you listen to the lies of satan offered to us in a cleverly disguised magazine article on beauty and self-worth? If we secure our self in the living Word of God, the Bible, and believe what

God says about who we are, we will find we are much more content and fulfilled and free in our lives. If the Bible influences our judgments about ourselves, then we can know true beautiful freedom. Yet if we look to the world, to satan, to define who we are, then we are going to get nothing but decay and sorrow. The world's beauty is fleeting; God's beauty is forever. We can never be free so long as we are believing lies about ourselves. For example if we choose to believe as the Bible says that we are God's handiwork, beautiful and good, created for a purpose (Ephesians 2:10), then we will live that out being free and secure. If we believe that we are ugly because we don't look like the skinny photoshopped, airbrushed model in the magazines, then we will act as though we are ugly hiding away and hoping we won't be seen, hating what we see in the mirror and believing everybody else hates us, too. It is a choice. In Deuteronomy 30:19, God says, "I have set before, life or death, blessings or curses, now choose life...." It is that choice we must make in everything—God's way or satan's way—life or death.

The enemy is in the world, and he is very subtle. satan can mix lies, deception, and distortion with just enough truth until we are drawn in and believe his way is truth. Once we believe what satan says about ourselves over what God says about us or look to satan's benchmark for how we should be instead of God's benchmark ideas, we are trapped. Sometimes we don't even realise how trapped we are. Once we allow satan's lies to take root in our lives, our freedom becomes compromised, and we must fight and choose freedom over death, truth over lies. We must look to the One who created us to tell us who we should be, who we are. We must be securely rooted in God's life-giving Word because through the Word blessing and freedom will flow. If we know how God wants us to live our life, we will know beautiful freedom.

Now I know that many of you reading this will say, "It's not that simple". No, in some ways it isn't. In some way it is a big battle. I will not deny the cost because there is a cost. It is an ongoing journey that can wear us down at times. I have been fighting for many years to find the freedom that Christ died for me to have. I constantly slip up and turn back to lies the world tells me about who I am, and yet there is no condemnation because Jesus never gives up. Freedom is always there, and in that I can constantly make the choice to turn back to the Word, pick up my Bible, and stand in the truth of His Word about me. That is the battle—to continually and constantly make that choice to hear and listen to the voice of God, the voice of truth. God's voice is and can break loudly into any brokenness. In the sight of the mighty roar of God, satan's feeble whisper must fall. Seek out the voice of God and stand firm in the fight.

That does not have to be as daunting as it sounds. You do not battle alone. We battle with Christ and in Christ, Holy Spirit is in us and "the One who is in you is greater than the one who is in the world!" (1 John 4:4). So it is with Christ. We battle and because of that we are sure to win, victory is already won, freedom is ours, Christ came, died and rose again for it. One of the most heartbreaking things is brokenness within Christians. As Christians we have freedom and so much authority to stand tall and brave in our freedom. The battle has already been won. It is a choice to win, and that choice can be broken down into simple choices

The first choice which comes after choosing to forgive, is to choose to want to be free. To choose to want live in all God has for you. To choose to want to be able to look in that mirror and like what you see, truly like what you see. In some way we all want that. We all long for freedom even if the fire has torn us down and the waves have killed us inside to the point that we give up believing life would ever change. Deep down we still long for freedom even when it seems impossible. In God it is possible. "It is for freedom that Christ has set us free, stand firm then, and do not let yourselves be burdened by a yoke of slavery." (Galatians 5:1).

God does not leave us alone, He will and has equipped you for the fight against satan. The fight for your soul here on Earth—the Kingdom of God. Remember your soul is your mind, your will and your emotions. That is where the battle starts.

It is time to say no to satan—No, no more!—and stand in your authority and inheritance as a believer and follower of Christ. It's time to believe the truth of who you are. You are a saint, fully secure and accepted in Christ and through Him. If you choose to make a choice to do what it takes for freedom, then God will honour you and come beside you shoulder to shoulder and you will find beautiful freedom.

CHAPTER TWELVE

EQUIPPED FOR THE FIGHT

While standing shoulder to shoulder with Jesus in the fight you do not stand alone. We stand ready for the fight fully secure in Him and fully equipped for the fight. We stand ready with the armour of God firmly in place and with our armour we win the fight. God has not asked you to equip yourself for the fight, He does that. The fight is against satan not against God and not against mankind. The fight is for our mind and our beliefs about ourselves. The fight is also for our spiritual life and our intimate relationship with God. God is so much bigger and more powerful than anything satan can throw at us, and without God we are weak. Alone we cannot withstand the fight. It is okay to be weak. It is okay to say we cannot do it. That does not make us a failure. It does not make us pathetic or useless. It makes us human and means we can look to God to help us in the fight.

We are complete in Christ Jesus, and that means we are above satan because of Jesus. The order of things is that God is higher than us, and then through Jesus we rise above satan who is lower than us. It is because of Jesus we can win against satan. Therefore, we are not weak when we are with Jesus. We have the same power that raised Christ from the grave within us, and that makes us above satan and so much more powerful than he is.

God knows we cannot fight all our pain, trials, and hardship alone. That is why He equips us for the fight. We read in the Bible about the armour of God, the armour God has given us and equipped us with to fight. Every piece of it is needed and every piece is given to every believer. The armour is securely in place from the moment we are saved. People often talk about "putting on" the armour of God as though picking up each item and dressing each morning. Putting on in this context means to choose to use. The armour is always on as a believer of Christ, and yet we often do not use our armour and then blame God when things don't go well.

We are in the fight with God, but we have to do it with Him. We have to make a choice to fight. We cannot sit around expecting God to simply do it all for us. He will do it *with* us but not *for* us. There are times where an instant divine healing happens, but those times are rare, and in most cases we have to do it with Him and through Him. When we are given the chance to use our armour of God and do so then we grow closer to God because we work through Him and in Him. It is an exciting journey, and we know satan has no chance of winning, but until we choose to use the tools and protection God gave us, satan will and can rob, steal, and destroy us. It is important to remember that satan "prowls around like a roaring lion looking for someone to devour" (1 Peter 5:8). The word *like* is very important in that sentence. satan is only *like* a roaring lion; he is not a roaring lion. Jesus is the lion, the Lion of Judah who roars with authority in the face of satan. satan is hoping we forget that he is only *like* a roaring lion, because he knows then we fear him, and when we fear him we do not fight, satan tricks us with lies, and and so he lets his lies then destroy our minds. Thus our mind itself becomes a battlefield. Sometimes it's not even that we fear satan when we let him win, but rather that we don't acknowledge him or his power and are therefore not always aware of the effects he has on us. So stand firm and stand ready for the fight, fully equipped and secure in Christ, and the battle will be won.

"Finally, be strong in the Lord and in His mighty power. Put on the full armour of God, so that you can take your stand against the devil's schemes. For our struggle is not against flesh and blood, but against the rulers, against the authorities, against the powers of this dark world and against the spiritual forces of evil in the heavenly realms. Therefore put on the full armour of God, so that when the day of evil comes, you may be able to stand your ground, and after you have done everything, to stand. Stand firm then, with the belt of truth buckled round your waist, with the breastplate of righteousness in place, and with your feet fitted with the readiness that comes from the gospel of peace. In addition to all this, take up the shield of faith, with which you can extinguish all the flaming arrows of the evil one. Take the helmet of salvation and the sword of the Spirit, which is the word of God. And pray in the Spirit on all occasions with all kinds of prayers and requests. With this in mind, be alert and always keep on praying for all the Lord's people" (Ephesians 6:10-18).

Here the Apostle Paul is encouraging the believers to stand against satan in the battle. The armour he describes is the Roman armour, which was familiar to the people, so that the people reading his letter would have been able to understand and relate to the different parts of the armour he was talking about. This r, however, is a spiritual armour, one that has been given to you to equip you. Often we learn and teach about the armour of God in our Sunday schools. We colour in pictures of a Roman soldier and somehow try to explain to our children that this is so much more than a physical armour, but very few people actually understand what that means, partly because very few people truly understand the battle we are in. Over the next few pages I am going to break down each piece of the armour and what that means for us in the spiritual battle, and how we can use the tools given to us in each piece. It's so important to understand that each of these pieces of armour are already on you. That's right: You already have them on. God has given them to you and never takes them off. We are the ones who forget they are there and forget to use them.

See each piece as a tool, and if we don't use the tools to help us be free from the bondage and brokenness we feel, then we can never be free. Each tool is important and valuable. Stand then ready with each tool God has given you, and over time you will find it easier as it becomes a natural thing to use your tools when hardship and difficulty come your way. It is overcoming that difficulty by using these tools which brings freedom to us.

The Belt of Truth

Jesus is truth, His words stand true and we read the truth in the Bible. satan is the prince of lies, and he will lie and tell us anything to rob us of our life, or any part of our life. satan will try any tactic to convince us that his ways are good and harmless. The Bible says he will present himself as an angel of light (2 Corinthians 11:14). We are told in the Bible that satan is very beautiful and attractive. "The truth will set you free" (John8:32). When a room is in darkness and we switch on the light, we see the room and everything in it so much more clearly than if we were trying to look around in the dark. That is what the truth is like. If we read our Bible we are literally bringing truth to lies—bringing light into the darkness.

The belt of truth is a very powerful tool that defeats satan, the father of lies. When you stand ready and use your belt of truth, you are shining light into satan's lies and showing them for what they really are—lies and deception. We can do this practically through a process called renewing the mind. The Bible tells us that we are transformed and set free by the renewing of our mind (Romans 12:2).

For so long I believed I was stupid. I struggled at school and was always in the bottom set. I could not get my head around the work and struggled to read and write properly. My teachers said I wouldn't get many GCSEs and it was unlikely that I would go on to higher education. The world and our society puts a heavy weight on success in career and academic achievement, and so satan began to convince me that I was stupid. For too long I had measured myself against others and come to the conclusion that I was stupid. satan's lies convinced me I was stupid because I let the lies tell me I was stupid, devalued, ugly, always alone, and many more. satan had no authority to tell me that but I let him when I believed him and did not call him a liar. I didn't look to the truth to define who I was. Had I looked in the truth of God's Word, I would have seen all the wonderful truths of who I am. I would have seen that I am made Christ-like and reflecting His image. I would have seen that I don't have to be perfect. I would have seen that God has called me beautiful. I would have known that I am never alone because God never leaves me. I would have known that I am not stupid. The belt of truth equips us to fight against satan's lies. The belt of truth equips us to fight for our mind and our thought-patterns so that we can align our thoughts to God's thoughts about us.

Jesus can restore all things. He is so loving, so

beautiful. He is our best friend. It is in Jesus that "the old has gone and the new has come" (2 Corinthians 5:17). So often we believe lies about ourselves. Maybe it's time to make this the time to dare to put down those thoughts that do not build us up and edify us as followers of Christ. For so long I thought I was ugly and stupid, and I could not seem to force myself to see it any other way. What I didn't understand is that because I believed something for so long it took time to unlearn that lie or that behaviour. When we start by using our belt of truth and the tools God gave us in His armour, we start to see a wonderful freedom.

Our words are powerful. What we say affects us and those around us, not just because we convince ourselves and others of what we are saying but because it effects the spiritual realms. What we say can either give satan a foothold or make him run from us. God is truth and speaks only truth. His living breathing Word is in the Bible. The Bible is not a dead book written 2,000 years ago but truly alive and not static, the Word of God. satan knows the Bible and he knows the truth, but he lies and deceives us by making his ways seem innocent, fun, and attractive.

satan also lies to us about who we are and who God is. To renew the mind, we need to cancel out all the lies. We cannot overcome a thought with another thought; we have to overcome a thought with a Word. God spoke the world into being with words (Genesis 1). With words Jesus calmed the storm (Mark 4:35-41). With words Jesus told the paralyzed man to pick up his mat and walk (Luke 5:18-25). Our words have effect, when we declare the truth of God with our mouths, it effects the spiritual realm for good just as when we declare the lies of satan it effects the spiritual realm negatively.

I found it really helpful to write down all the negative things that are not things of God that I believed about myself, the things that were not truth of what God would say about me. Then with prayer and help from others, I found a truth from the Bible that counteracted that lie. I wrote the truth out, and every time that negative thought came into my mind I was able to beat it with a truth.

Here are a few examples:

The lie said: God gets fed up with me and leaves me.

Yet God's truth told me: The Lord will not reject me and will never abandon me: Psalm 94:14.

The lie said: I am stupid.

God's truth told me: The Lord gives me skillful and Godly wisdom: Proverbs 2:6.

The lie said: I am not allowed to cry.

God's truth told me: There is a time for me to cry: Ecclesiastes 3:4.

I did this with all the lies from satan and I still do. I have them all stuck up in my flat, on my mirror, in my kitchen cupboards; anywhere I would be reminded of God's truth about me. Whenever those old lies or new ones, come into my mind, I am able to declare God's truth into that lie. satan cannot stand before God's truth. satan's lies have no place before God's truth and he knows it, thus he begins to lose his grip on your thoughts. Though at first it feels like saying over and over stuff you do not believe, it *is* truth and even satan knows it is truth. Over time as the light of truth is brought into the situation, one little bit at a time, there will come a point when there is more light in your thoughts and in you than darkness. This is what we call freedom. It is possible to get to a point where we have more light than darkness in us. Though it is not easy, over time freedom will come. Keep declaring the truth of God's Word over yourself and over others, and soon you will see the beautiful effects in your life and theirs. Don't declare satan's lies over yourself or others, even for a joke. satan does not care if was a joke or not when you said your friend is an idiot, satan takes it and uses it, it is a curse. As the Bible says "We demolish arguments and every pretension that sets itself up against the knowledge of God, and we take captive every thought to make it obedient to Christ" (2 Corinthians 10:5). We do this practically in the way I have just explained by renewing the mind. Don't let the bad thought even land, as soon as you believe something that is against God, take it captive by declaring it as a lie, then make it obedient to Christ, by declaring the truth of God's Word.

I am not saying it is all perfect for me now. There are days when I feel I am stupid. That is a lie that still holds me sometimes. There are days when I wake up and feel like everything I do is wrong. Yet deep down I know the truth, and out of my mouth I declare the truth of God and His Word and I do not feel condemned for it. Sometimes though I don't, sometimes I speak out the lies. Those are the days when I am not standing firm with my belt of truth. Don't blame yourself when you declare negative things. When I do, I say "sorry" to God and simply at that point make a choice to declare His truth. His truth is more powerful than any negativity I've said, and so in the spiritual realm blessings from God have more power than the curses we say.

We are literally blessing or cursing ourselves with our words. Ask Jesus to show you the lies you believe about yourself and to show you the truth so that you can renew your mind to His way. Ask Jesus to be with you and protect your mind from the lies of satan.

Sometimes it can also help if you say a prayer to renounce the lies you have believed and spoken over yourself. To renounce is more than just saying sorry for saying those lies. To renounce is to remove the spiritual authority that lie gave satan in your life. This is a way of telling God that you are choosing to let go of those lies. That does not mean that you will stop believing them overnight or that God's truth will take root in you overnight. It does mean that you want to choose blessings over curses. That is part of what it means to choose life—to renounce the lies you speak into the spiritual realm.

You can say a simple prayer for each lie and declare each truth, such as:

Lord Jesus, thank You that You love me and that You tell me the truth in Your Word. I renounce the lie that says _____ and I choose to believe Your truth that _____. Thank You for Your love and grace. Amen.

The Breastplate of Righteousness

To be righteous means to be right before God. Sinners cannot be right before God because sin is not of God. God cannot look at sin and sin cannot be in Heaven. The great news is as believers we are not sinners—we are saints! God doesn't look at us and see sinners. He looks at us and sees saints through the act of love Jesus took on the cross. Therefore this means we are righteous because we have accepted Jesus and what He did on the cross. We have accepted righteousness—not our own righteousness but Christ's righteousness. Saints are righteous, and we are saints. Yes, we sin. We are human and we mess up. As I said earlier, sin is separation from God. But it is not God who separates because God looks at us as righteous. It is we who turn away from God when we sin. It is we who say to God that we would rather go another way, satan's way. It is we who move away from God when we choose to sin.

This turning away does not make us sinners because we are saved saints and God always looks at us as though we are righteous, because we are, transformed and redeemed in Christ. We are righteous. When we accepted Jesus as our Saviour, we stopped being sinners and our sinner's clothes were changed and the breastplate of righteousness was given to us. God never takes that righteousness away. We always wear the breastplate. Yet when sinning we turn from God and walk farther and farther away from Him. That is how the separation occurs as we move, not God. God holds steadfast looking towards us with open arms like the prodigal son's father waiting for us to turn back and come home to Him. We do this by admitting what we have done and coming back to God and confessing and telling Him we are sorry. When we do that He is there as a loving Father with His arms open wide waiting for us to return. He embraces us and smiles. He never took the breastplate of righteousness from us. So we never stopped being righteous, but when we turn our back on God the breastplate, which shields our front, stops facing God. When we turn back to Him our breastplate that comes from Jesus faces God again and that is what He sees. He sees our righteousness.

It is a choice to admit that you have done wrong, turn back to God, say sorry, and then try not to do it again because each time you do you turn your back to God again. If you do continue to sin, however, do not fear because God never turns away or gives up. He is always there with His arms open wide waiting and longing for you to turn back to Him. He gives you free will. You have a choice to turn from Him and He will not stop you, though He will long for you to return to Him.

For the Roman soldier the breastplate protects the

heart. The soul—our mind, will and emotions—is sometimes called the heart. Our righteousness is what protects our soul from the attack. We are righteous before God therefore our soul is righteous and protected in Him.

Here is a prayer you could say if you want to say sorry to God for your sin and turn back to Him:

Father God, Thank You for Your love and grace. Thank You that You care about me so much that You sent Jesus to die for me. I am sorry for _____. Thank You that You have made me righteous before Jesus. Amen.

The Shoes of Peace

The gospel is the good news that Jesus died for you, and rose again to defeat satan. Through that beautiful act of love He has forgiven you and cleansed you of your sins. He gives you a peace and an assurance. Because of what Jesus did on the cross you can be assured of yourself and of the truth and your faith in Him. Through the Spirit of Peace that is the filling of Holy Spirit in your life, you can feel at rest in Him. In trials and difficulty, anxiety and worry, you can stand firm with peace in your heart because no matter what happens or what you do, the good news of the gospel is that God loved you so much that He sent His Son to die for you.

When worry and anxiety fill us we can stand in peace and rest assured that Jesus is on our side because He died to give us safety and peace. I know that sounds much simpler than it feels, but we can start to feel it. The next time anxiety comes choose to say, "In Jesus I have peace, I have the Spirit of Peace in me". Take a deep breath and ask Jesus to be with you and fill you with His peace. It is possible, and once you are filled with His peace and assured that He died for you, you can rest in His good news. It is because we are in joy and peace of the good news that Jesus died for us that we are able and asked by God to take this news to all who need to hear it. God has equipped us to do it, and in peace we are able to share with others that Jesus died to set them free.

Peace equips us in the battle because it is with anxiety and worry that satan will try to attack. Fear keeps us enslaved to satan's ways. With the shoes of Peace we can tell the spirit of anxiety and fear which is of satan to go. Those negative spirits must leave us.

God has equipped us with a deep peace for the fight, and has enabled us to share the news of the good news with peace in our heart.

When anxiety and fear attack here is a simple prayer

you can pray out loud to declare the Spirit of Peace into the situation:

Jesus, fill me with Your peace because you have equipped me to fight. In the name of Jesus Christ of Nazareth fear and anxiety have no place in me. I am in Jesus and in His authority. Amen.

The Shield of Faith

When satan sends his lies and his attacks like fiery arrows at us and we face trails and difficulty, we can stand with the shield of faith and those attacks will bounce off of us. We have faith in the sovereign King. God is the Most High God who can extinguish all attacks and difficulties. God can overcome all suffering and adversity. We have faith that He will save us, that He will heal us from the sickness we carry. A few years ago I found out there was something medically wrong with my uterus. It was a very painful and quite a difficult time for me. I found out that there is a chance I will never be able to have children. As a woman in my early 20s I could not make sense of it. Though at the time I wasn't even in a place to consider children, as I have grown older, even though I am not married I find it difficult to know that it is a distinct possibility that I will never have children.

Though there is a small chance I could carry

children with my uterus as it is, it is unlikely. I could wait and see or I could pray and desire God's healing or I could accept my situation. In that difficult situation, I can choose to raise my shield of faith and declare, "I have faith God will heal me... but even if He doesn't I still have faith in Him...." It's in that *even if he doesn't* moment that we find true protection from the fiery arrows. Having faith in who God is and His ability to heal me does not change my situation with my uterus, nor does it mean that I am suddenly okay with it. It does mean that I am fully secure in who God is and in my trust in Him. I have faith that He will heal me because it says so in His Word, and there is no sickness in the Kingdom of God, but even if He doesn't heal my uterus until I am restored in Heaven, I still have faith and trust in who He is.

By saying that, I put up my shield of faith and that trial, that difficulty, does not ruin or damage my relationship with God, and actually I then no longer feel as affected by that difficult situation because I am resting in my faith in God for my security and healing.

When we go through difficult times, such as losing a job or a relationship breakdown, we can raise our shield of faith and say, "God will help me get me a new job.... But even if He does not, my faith in Him is not dependent on a new job....." That affirms that satan cannot succeed in destroying our relationship with God or our faith in who He is. My relationship and faith in God is not dependent on the healing of my uterus.

Two things I hate for people to say to me are: "He never puts you through more than you can bear" and "He puts us through stuff for a reason". No! God never ever put me through my pains and struggles, and He never put you through yours either. Please don't let that lie enter your head. Yes, God uses the bad things for good. I would not be able to write this book and serve Him the way I do if I had not been through the things I have been through. I am who I am today because of the struggles I have faced. But God did not want me to go through the struggles I went through. God's heart cried for my pain and my brokenness just as mine did. God wept for all I have had to face, and He wept for all you have had to face.

At times I felt that I could not bear the things I have felt. I know many people who couldn't bear what they have been through. That is not the issue. This issue is that God is there with us and is the One who helps us to bear what we have been through. He is the One who carries us through. It is because of God and His love that we are able to bear the things we go through. That is the hope. That is the joy. Do not let go of that hope. Be patient and keep your eyes on Jesus, for He is your healing path. Raise your shield of faith and declare into your pains that God will save you but even if He doesn't you will not stop having faith in who He is. Through that, satan's arrows of fire will never get close to you! It is so easy to give up on God when struggles come. In those times rise your shield of faith and declare He is God.

The Helmet of Salvation

Our salvation is secure as our names are written in the Lamb's Book of Life and our names are never blotted out. Once we accept Jesus Christ as our Lord and saviour, and accept His act on the cross our names are written in the book of life for all eternity. Salvation is our eternal life in Heaven. Once we accepted what Jesus did on the cross for us, there is no question in the Spiritual realm about our salvation. satan knows that we are saved, and God knows we are saved. But we often question our salvation. We sometimes wonder if we really are saved and really will go to Heaven. Each time we sin we can have the tendency to think this means we have lost our salvation. We end up seeing forgiveness from God as a way of getting our salvation back, and thus if we sin and forget to say we are sorry we will not go to Heaven. It's not like that. Our salvation is set, and our names will never be blotted out. Our eternity in Heaven is secure from the moment we accept Jesus. This does not mean we can just go out and sin like it doesn't matter because it does. As I have said before, by sinning we are still separated from God and satan is trying to destroy our life now. Once we accepted Jesus we entered the Kingdom of God. The Kingdom of God is now. satan knows that our weakness is our thoughts and our minds, and so he attacks our minds to try to convince us that we are not saved. satan tries to convince us of lies about who God is and who we are by trying to convince us that because we sin we lose our salvation because God is an angry God. No! God is so loving that He died for our eternal salvation.

satan attacks our minds, and so when those lying thoughts about our salvation come, we can stand in the knowledge and assurance of what Jesus did for us on the cross by holding firm to the truth of our salvation. The helmet of our salvation prevents those lies from penetrating our minds. Wear your helmet of salvation as protection for your mind.— Believe in the truth that you are saved. Don't let satan's lies rob you of your freedom in Christ the King who died for your salvation.

As with the belt of truth, when the lies come, any

lies send them away with the truth, declare the truth that you are saved, and rest assured that you will be in eternity with Christ.

If you have not yet accepted Jesus as your Lord and saviour and feel now like you want to do so, or if you want to reaffirm to Jesus your commitment to Him here is a prayer you could say:

Jesus, Thank You that you died on the cross, and rose again for me. Thank You that you love me so much. I have sinned but I choose to accept your grace and salvation. Today I commit myself to you as a believer and follower of you. I stand firm in my salvation. Amen.

The Sword of the Spirit

Holy Spirit will smash any stronghold and tear down any obstruction. God's Holy Spirit lives inside of you and moves from you and through you. Every one of us wrestles with strongholds in our lives. These are things that trap us and keep us in chains. Strongholds can be birthed out of our own words and declarations. I spent most of my teen years vowing I would never be weak. I vowed I would be strong. I declared that vow by saying, "I will not be weak; I will not cry." It became such a stronghold in me that I actually stopped crying—at least about the things that matter. If I did cry I felt weak and useless

206

because I couldn't even keep my own promises and my own vows. This vow took root in me and I felt numb inside myself. I hungered after the feeling of being numb inside because I felt good that way and felt almost human in my distorted idea of what it was to be human. I thought emotions were bad and to be numb felt freeing.

When I was numb I felt acceptable because I had no emotions, which I thought were weak. What happened in me, however, was that all the good and Godly emotions were lost, and I was left with anger, rage, hate, confusion, sadness, guilt, and shame. That *feeling weak because of my emotions* was a stronghold that grew in me until slowly over time I reached the point where I could not seem to let go of vows I made and could not seem to break free from their bondage.

Vows such as "I will never love again" or "I will never call a church home again" or "I will never trust a vicar" are vows I made, and at the time intended to keep. satan uses theses vows to trap us because when we speak these words they have power, and satan takes them as permission. We should never say such vows even as a joke because like with curses satan does not care if it was a joke or not, he takes them as permission to trap us in these strongholds. Strongholds not only trap us in death and guilt but can grow fruit in our life that is moldy and ungodly. They hinder our relationship with God and His people. When I vowed I would never call a church home again I put spiritual blockages in place to stop me from belonging in my church.

Strongholds can also come from situations or circumstances from our past. Strongholds are what satan uses to stop us being free warriors of Christ. I for many years have been trapped in the stronghold that *I will mess up so badly that people will kick me out of a group or church and stop talking to me.* I have been bound by this stronghold for years. I have worried constantly if I would end up loosing all my friends or being kicked out of the group of people. Strongholds are chains that bind.

We believers do not have to worry or fear, though, because we have the sword of the Spirit. God's Spirit can smash through any chains that bind. God's Spirit can set us free from the strongholds that trap us. We do this practically through prayer and worship. God's Spirit resides in us, and His Word is in the Bible but also moving in us and through us. Our words our powerful, and when we pray in the Spirit (and I am not just talking of praying in tongues) we are aligning with God to break through every chain that binds. Our words through our prayers are worship. With God's Spirit the words we speak are so sharp, as a sword, and so on fire that no work of satan can remain. To pray God's words, words that align yourself to God, words that declare authority and freedom over strongholds, is praying in the Spirit, which is using the sword of the Spirit.

By choosing to rejoice and praise and thank God even in the difficult times and declaring over and over that He will smash every chain, by declaring satan has no authority over our bodies and using our words to bring freedom is moving in the sword of the spirit. Stand tall, raise your hands in worship, and thank God for your freedom in Christ Jesus. When you do that satan must run from you and every chain of bondage will be smashed before you. In your darkness praise the Lord. In your worry and fear tell satan to get away from you because he has no place near you because you are in the authority of Christ Jesus. You are complete in Jesus and free in Him. By declaring these truths you are declaring it into the spiritual realms and allowing the sword of the Spirit to break you free into more of the life Christ died for you to have. This is also why praise and worship in the Lord is so vitally important.

To break the vows and the strongholds, we must first repent of and renounce those vows. To repent of them means to admit you said them and that they were wrong and to ask God for forgiveness. To renounce means to lay down and give up and take back the spiritual authority they gave to satan, and so to renounce a vow with the Spirit of God is to break its authority over you. It doesn't have to be a big thing. The church is very good at making out these sorts of things as big and huge, but they are not.

Here is a simple prayer you can say if you want to break certain vows or promises you have made. It maybe good to have a trusted, spiritually mature friend with you when you say it, so that they can pray for you as you do. Remember that Jesus is bigger than satan and so there is nothing to fear. Jesus is with you and walks with you:

Jesus, thank You that You love me so much, thank You that through You I can be restored. I am sorry for the vow I made that said _____ .
Thank You that You have forgiven me. In Your name Jesus I renounce this vow and declare that in Your Spirit it has no authority over me. Thank You for Your love. Amen.

However, the sword of the Spirit is not for you to go looking for a fight, but it is a flaming, sharp sword that comes from the Word of God. Holy Spirit is within you and He is moving mightily. Allow Him to move in you, through you, and for you. Stand in prayer, stand in worship, and rejoice and thank the

Lord no matter what. The Spirit of God will win any battle. He will break any chains because where He is there is freedom.

CHAPTER THIRTEEN

BREAK EVERY CHAIN

satan's ways are powerful and do have power behind them. There are many ways that he wants to trap you. We are in a culture so very interested in spirituality, yet any spirituality that is not God's affects us negatively without our even realising it. I will not deny satan has power, and while I wholeheartedly agree and rejoice in the fact that God's ways are more powerful than satan's ways, I acknowledge that satan does have power and desires to trick us into giving him the authority over our lives. Yes, of course, Jesus has the authority over satan and so do we as we have Holy Spirit inside of us, so we need not fear the ways of satan, but we do need to be aware of them. It is a very real battle, and satan will use any tactic he has at his disposal to trick us into his path.

There are more and more new age shops in our towns. Psychics and tarot card readers, charging premium prices are commonplace in our shopping centres, and people more and more are turning to satan to fulfill a need that God can fulfill, but only if we let Him. People are looking to eastern spiritualties through yoga, karma, tai-chi, healing massages, reiki healing, crystals, mindfulness, aromatherapy, and acupuncture. All of these are rooted in a spirituality that is not God's. These things "work." reiki healing does heal. Acupuncture works. Yet they heal through the power of satan not the power of God. satan wants you to believe these are good ways to get healing, which is why he uses his power to heal so that you will be drawn in by it because spiritually you end up opening yourself up to more than you intended. You open yourself to satan's ways and thus bring spiritual death on yourself.

Tarot card readers and phychics and horoscopes can tell you extremely accuate futures, but they do this through communication with demons. God and His Holy Spirit can prophesy life into our lives, and yet people turn to death for our fortunes coming from satan. It is important to stay rooted in God's path. God has all the power, all the answers, all the healing and restoration we need. You don't want the fake or the counterfeit spirituality that satan gives you. You want the genuine God who genuinely heals and restores. satan's healing will only bring healing for a short while but open other parts of our body to his ways, usually spiritually. Be aware and pray, asking Jesus what's right to be involved in or to read before doing it, especially if it is in the area of spirituality and healing.

Keep your eyes on Jesus, the way to see if something is fake or counterfeit is to know the genuine thing. To recognise satan's counterfeit ways is not to look at satan but to look at Jesus. When we know truth we spot a lie straight away.

While I recogise there is something spiritually dangerous to do with intentionally looking for healing in these counterfeit ways, however we must remember satan tricks. The Bible is clear he lies, he comes dressed as an angel of light. he does not care if we *knew* it was tapping into his demonic realm or not. Yes Jesus has authority over satan but by getting involved in satan's occult ways we give him the authority into our lives, mind and body, even if we did not know what we were doing.

Maybe you are reading this and you know you have been or are involved in some of these things. Don't worry. God still has authority and is still in you and with you. You may want to find somebody you know and trust who understands these things to talk it through with, but it is also possible to say a simple prayer to renounce the things you have been involved in:

Jesus, thank You that You died for me on the cross. Thank You that You love me so much that You overcame satan so that I can be free. I am sorry that I have been involved in _____. Thank You that Your Spirit and power is so much bigger than satan. I renounce my involvement in _____ and thank You for Your loving protection and cleansing and healing. Amen.

Again these things don't need to be big or scary because we just need to stand in the authority of Christ because He is in us. We do all things in Him. We shake off the old way because of His power and we find a new way. When we seek His way, He will show it to us.

This is important: **Do not** go looking for the ways of satan. Not even to try to understand what I am talking about here. Keep your eyes on God. Don't go looking on Google for the things I have mentioned because the darkness of satan is attractive and addictive and ensnares many. Talk with somebody you know about these things and trust in what the loving Lord has to say to you. I pray wholeness, protection, and Godly wisdom on your life now as you seek after the life Christ died for you to have.

Generational curses and blessings.

One of my favorite verses in the Bible and the one the title of this book is based on is Deuteronomy 30:19: "I have set before you life and death, blessings and curses, now choose life so that you and your children may live." I find this verse to be so profound on so many levels. It explains so clearly how freedom is a choice. We are literally making a choice between life and death when we choose God's ways over satan's way, but it is not just for us that we make the choice but for our children also. I don't have any children and perhaps never will, but I want to make a choice for life now, I want to choose life so that any children I do have or any people I will interact with or minister to in the future can also have life. We affect those around us and generationally we pass things on to the generations below us. In the Bible we read about the blessings or curses being passed on to the generations below us. This is a very misunderstood passage and can often be used to hurt and even abuse people. I have met people whose lovely children have been born with an illness or disability and others who have had miscarriages or still births and been told by Christians that these were a curse because of their sin. No, this is wrong— so very wrong. If you have been told something like this, I am sorry. This is so very wrong. It saddens me that Christian people still believe such things. Your children are beautiful and precious.

This verse in Exodus is talking about behaviours we have that will be copied and learnt by our children or those around us we minister to and look up to. Recently I was told that certain people are looking to me because they see me as spiritually mature. This surprised me because I had always seen myself as the one who's broken and needs help from others. I realised then that if people are looking to me to see God and to learn to live in the way God wants, then they will learn from my behaviour just as children do.

I have been known to be quite angry and rude, quite blunt, and to snap at people when I do not like things or things are not the way I want them. I can be quite sure I am right and determined to put forward my opinion firmly. The root of that is that I feel stupid and told myself I'm stupid for so long that I am determined to feel like I know something and that I feel my opinion is valued. The problem— the *truth*—is that I was never stupid. I always was quite clever and astute to the world around me. I notice things others would just pass by without a second thought. I am incredibly aware of spiritual things and study and understand the Bible very well. I have learnt that I don't need to push my point or have everyone agree with me to be clever. That behaviour came out of a lie from satan and was only bringing death to me. Had those around me learnt that behaviour, and if I had children as their mother they would copy me? I would have passed that behavior on. This is what Exodus is referring to when it talks about curses' being passed on. Curses passed to our children are those negative attitudes, values, and behaviors our children learn and copy.

Yet we can break that. We can change. As it says in Deuteronomy we can choose life so that we and our children may live. When I began to deal with the lie that says I'm stupid, when I stopped declaring that over myself and chose to say I have good and Godly wisdom, I found that those angry, aggressive, and determined behaviours in me diminished. I was calmer and able to share my wisdom for the right reasons and in the right way not just so that I could prove to myself I was clever. I began to pray and ask God if correcting somebody when I knew I was right was the right thing to do, or to just let it be because sometimes it's not important, and always correcting somebody puts them down to make me feel good. I learnt that if God was saying it is important to share my wisdom then I needed to do it in a way that was not rude or devaluing of others. It was a new learnt behaviour that I had to learn over many years.

Though now I know that doing this has brought life not only into my life and those around me and in my friendships and relationships, but also into the lives of those who look up to me or any children I may have in the future, who will learn and copy these new and Godly ways of reacting. In that way I will no longer pass on the curses—learnt negative behavior—to my children but will instead pass on the blessings—learnt Godly behavior. This is why it is important to choose life and break down any strongholds. By choosing life we live a better and healthier spiritual life, but it also means our children or future children will have blessings through our choosing to be healed in Him.

If you think of some behaviours your parents or grandparents had that you picked up and learnt, you can often see this pattern in yourself. If you have children, you can look at them and see yourself in them. This is what generational blessings and curses are. Choose life.

If you see behaviours in yourself from your parents or in your children from you that are a negative way of reacting or doing things and you see it bringing death to yourself or to them, you can break this stronghold and ask God to help you release blessings into your life and theirs:

Lord, thank You for loving me and giving me the tools and power to break any stronghold. I have identified the generational behaviour of _____ in myself/my children. I renounce this stronghold and ask that You allow Your blessings to flow through me into my children. Amen.

Communion.

Communion is a beautiful act of unity and community, which is the Lord's meal. We can all share in the beautiful communion together because we are one in Christ. Jesus said in the last supper that we are to take communion to remember what He has done for us. To take communion, which is to share consecrated bread and wine together, is a symbol that we acknowledge and accept what Jesus did for us on the cross. By taking communion we accept that Jesus was tortured and humiliated and had a way out, He could choose to stop it but He didn't, He endured agonizing pain for us. Torture is horrific but anyone being tortured would stop if they could, choosing not to stop it when He could is the real torture of the cross of Jesus. He chose that to give us the grace of God, which is that we are forgiven and our sins are atoned for, restoring that intimate relationship with us God intended. By taking communion we accept that through Jesus we are changed and become as righteous as Jesus. He looks at us as saints. Jesus sacrificed Himself to rise again so that satan would be defeated and no longer have claim to our eternity. Jesus died as a beautiful act of love He could not stand to leave our relationship with God destroyed so much that He came to Earth for the sole purpose of restoring our relationship with God. We can accept communion as a symbol of love and restoration of our relationship with God.

Communion is also a symbol of the unity of the church. When we share in the one body and the one blood of the One who saved us all, we are becoming the complete bride in Him in unity. To symbolise and share in the unity of the body, we must be in unity to share communion together. Therefore it is important to restore any broken relationships with those in the church with whom you are about to share communion before doing so. It is not right to share communion, and therefore act as though you are in unity with others, if you are not. It is not right to share communion with others if you are holding anger and bitterness in your heart against another you are sharing communion with.

How can you accept the grace of God and the spiritual cleansing of the blood if you are harbouring unforgiveness towards somebody in the church?

Restore your relationships before coming to communion together. Forgive those in your heart you are angry with before coming to the communion table as an act of accepting your forgiveness, and unity of God's church. By being in unity before each other and before God, an amazing spiritual encounter will take place. To be in communion with each other is an act of forgiving and moving in unity as one body. We are one body made whole by the sharing of the one bread. If you are not in one accord with each other, if you are in discord and blame, it is right to make unity between you and that person before sharing in one body and blood of Jesus.

It might be that it is right to make peace in your heart, especially if the others are unaware of your feelings towards them. Let Jesus restore what is broken. Let Him cleanse you and let Him be the restorer of lives and relationships. When we talk about sharing a cup it is not always literally. Some churches are so big that more than one cup is used during the communion service. It is not right to say that because you are in discord with another you will just make sure you go to another cup. No, it's all one cup because they were both consecrated from the same prayer and symbolise the same act of Jesus. Sometimes coming to communion together and sharing in one cup is a way of saying to God that a disagreement or fallout has been resolved. This way you are saying to each other and to God that you are in unity with one another and that any issues have been resolved and laid to rest.

Communion in itself is healing. By taking communion something spiritual happens inside of us. The body and blood of Jesus are very powerful in the spiritual realm. By taking communion we literally join with Jesus. satan has the right to the eternity of sinners, yet Jesus defeated satan and through Him we are no longer sinners but saints. Jesus' blood sets us free and cleanses anything from darkness, including and especially us, because by the shedding of Jesus' blood and then rising again satan was defeated. Jesus' blood is so powerful that satan cannot be where the blood of Jesus is.

When we take the body and blood of Jesus inside of us by taking communion, it has an impact on our body spiritually because we align with Jesus, and through His blood satan and his demons cannot stay in us. When we take communion we are taking a spiritual cleansing of ourselves. I know myself that when I take communion I find freedom and release spiritually. In the spiritual realm, through the blood of Jesus we are accepting a deep cleansing, which is healing and freeing. When we take communion we are actually moving things massively in the spiritual realm. We are waging a battle, and before the blood of Jesus satan must run. The blood of Jesus seals any healing and destroys any strongholds. It is the blood of Jesus that cleanses. Let Jesus work in you as you take communion.

CHAPTER FOURTEEN

TEARS OF HEALING

The more we understand how to communicate with God, the deeper we will grow in relationship with Him. This is not an overnight job, and the journey to freedom is little steps at a time. It is about being in communication with God, getting to know Him, one step at a time. We need to spend time with Him. Often we struggle with prayer because it can feel like He's not there or is not listening, but know that He is. Try talking to Him. It doesn't have to be a very fancy prayer with lots of words. Just tell Him how you are and be honest with Him. If you are angry and want to be angry at Him, that's okay. He is okay with anger and with mess. If you are hurt or upset tell Him. That is okay. He has come to heal and restore your anger, mess, pain, and sadness. Tell Him how your day was and what your desires are. Just chat with Him as you would with any other friend. He cares. He wants to know about your day and about your life.

It is important to remember that it is God who is your hope, it's God who restores and heals you. You cannot do it alone, others cannot do it for you, and no program or church can fix you. But you and God working together at your freedom is a mighty thing. Don't look for the quick fix. Remember that this is a process that could take time. You have years of hurt and learnt behaviours to undo. Trust that each step along the way God is there and He will be shaping and transforming you as you go. So do not feel down or disheartened when it's not an instant process. It isn't that we work for however many months or years and stay completely unchanged, and then one day we wake up and it's the end and we are free and everything is sorted. Everything works more like a journey where each little thing is changed in us as we go on and grow deeper in revelation of who God is and who we are in Him.

Remember that there is a time for you to cry. Tears are not weak. God created us as emotional beings, and emotions are wonderful things. When you try to hide from what the world calls bad emotion and always be the joyful, happy, perfect person, you trap yourself in a prison you weren't designed to be in. God made you to be emotional, and your emotions are beautiful and very complex. It is really healing and freeing to feel emotions. Tears have wonderful healing properties. When we cry we actually let out the pain we feel inside, and by letting it out we accept what makes us sad and through that we can heal from it. You are never too emotional. There is no such thing. We are made to be emotional. The word emotional encompasses all sorts of beautiful and joyous emotions, including tears. Don't see tears as weak and don't try to suppress your emotions. I tried so hard for so many years to be what I thought was strong, which in my mind really meant *not crying*.

The trouble is that it is impossible to fully suppress all emotion, and so we stop feeling love and joy and feel emotions like anger, rage, fear, and bitterness, which fill the gap—and these emotions only seek to destroy you. These emotions come from satan. Tears are not negative. Our society tries to tell us it is not okay to cry because crying is somehow weak and negative. That is not true. We are not designed to bottle up our pain or our joy. Tears are a Godly natural reaction to the sadness and pains we feel as well as a beautiful reaction to the joy we feel. It is quite common for people to say they will not cry again. But if we suppress our tears for a long time we find it is so hard for us to cry because satan will happily take our tears from us if we give them to him, which we do when we suppress them. When he does take our tears it gives us a distorted idea of strength, bravery, and wholeness. The more we cry, the more healed and whole we are because we give voice and expression to our pain. satan is the one who convinces you that tears make you broken so that you will suppress them which is not a Godly way of dealing with pain. This is the same for all emotions. We are not made to suppress our emotions, it is impossible and when we try to we trap ourselves.

To face your pain and allow the tears to be released is so very healing. Often we fear if we cry we won't be able to stop. We are always able to stop, but we cannot know freedom and healing from our hurts and pains until we accept them and allow the emotions to be felt. Tears really are a gift of healing from God. If you have locked away your tears for so long you may find it hard to cry again, because through suppressing your emotions satan has traped you. Yet Jesus can open that trap and bring healing into anything. Try asking Jesus to help you cry again. Ask Jesus for the beautiful gift of tears. When you feel the need to cry, don't hold back. You will be surprised by the amount of healing your tears will bring you. It is healthier to cry than to bottle it all up. To release tears into a situation can be like letting go and letting out a healing balm into a situation that otherwise seems hopeless. Give your pain its outlet in tears.

Tears are also a way of expressing deep joy or gratitude. I often cry for all the Lord has done in my life. I find tears flow from me each time I achieve new things. I am constantly in awe of what the Lord has done, and it brings me to tears. This reveals that I am not weak or emotionally unstable but emotionally stable.

Tears are an incredibly beautiful thing. It is the braver thing to cry because it means you are accepting how you are feeling and allowing yourself to be in that, which runs against the world's way of doing things.

It is important to find a small number of people you trust to open up to, even just one person at first, because we are not made to do this journey alone. Many people have come alongside me, and each has played a part in my journey. I know that over the last 12 years, since the day I stood in Tanzania and decided to choose freedom, I have *never* been alone on that journey. It has not always been smooth after making that choice, and I hurt those who did come alongside me and have hurt my family over the years, but I have never been alone. Some amazing people have chosen to walk we me and what seemed to be a hopeless journey for my healing. I was always trying to do it alone, trying to survive and never letting anyone in but I couldn't survive. We need to be in community as the body of Christ. Our society is a very individualistic society that teaches us that we must be self-sufficient because we are told that self-sufficient means strength. We are taught to see asking for help and admitting we struggle as weakness.

I remember meeting somebody some years back, for hours and hours, week after week because Jesus had told me they could help me. I was desperate for help, yet I was afraid to tell them why I needed help. I sat in silence in front of that person, for hours never quite able to speak aloud my pain, yet desperate to speak out. The fear and shame trapped me. satan used that to take my words from me. It took a long time before I could speak and share my pain with that person because I was so afraid. I was afraid of the shame, I was afraid of how weak I thought it was to confide in others and I was afraid to admit what had been a deep-rooted brokenness. Yet as Jesus promised, with Him, when I was able to speak out my pain to that person, it became such a healing ministry. I took back my voice from satan and I gave the pain its voice. I found freedom in that. Our pain has a voice and only in Jesus, when we give the pain its voice and in its anger and tears can we release it and step into freedom and wholeness.

Blocking our voice and our emotions till we hide the reality of what we feel is so distorted, and not what God intended for us. It is *not* weak to say you need help. It is a very brave thing to say that something in your life is not right. It is very brave to say that even to yourself, and admitting it to somebody else is even braver. Do not think you have to heal life's hurts on your own. Nor do you have to fix it, it is okay to feel broken, God fixes all things. We often end up feeling like we have to give the set answer of "I'm fine, thanks" when somebody asks how we are even when really we are breaking down inside. We are very good at the "I'm fine, thanks" answer in churches, which is the answer that reaffirms that it is not okay to be anything other than fine. It is only when we are able to be open and honest about how we really feel with those we trust that we can truly find freedom from it.

God did not make us to be alone. As I said before it's not that we need to trust people right away. Trust is earned. But it is important to be able to admit to somebody how hurting you are and that you need help to find healing. It is important to hear this: It's okay; it is okay to feel broken; it is okay to need help; it is okay to cry. We all experience difficulty and hardship, much of it far out of our control, but we have a God who loves us and cares about us and who does not want us to face it alone. With your trusted person you can work through the things I have talked about in this book.

While it is an individual journey between you and God and it is only God who heals, it is something that you need to do with others alongside you. I will always be forever grateful for the wonderful Godly people who have played some part in my journey to healing and freedom. While it was not those people who healed me, I certainly could not have done it without them. We are designed to work with others. I have wonderful loving parents who care deeply for me and a big sister who has always looked out for me. My parents didn't give up on me when things went wrong because they cared. Each and every person who has played a part in my journey is special to me, even the ones I ended up hurting. God knew who I needed and what kind of ministry I needed at each time. Some have been strict in a firm approach, calming my anger and rebellious behaviour with consequences and firm boundaries, yet so loving and so willing to withstand anything to prove they will always stand beside me. Others strict yet loving with displaying the gentle compassion of Christ. Yet others holding steadfast, prayer warriors, who's consistant, steadfast prayers have broken into so much darkness and strongholds from satan for my freedom. Others offering the caring hand of friendship going out for drinks and and putting up with my childish, confused reactional responses, determined to show they were staying by me to see freedom in my life. My heart is full of gratitude to those who have walked a difficult journey to see my freedom, many of whom over the last 12 years I do not even see anymore, but I know that if I did they would smile for who I am today. I know I stand free because of the body of Christ. Every relationship is for a season. Yet each at the right time Jesus has brought to play a part in my freedom. It was Jesus who saved me, let's not confuse that, but it was His people who traveled that journey with me, and still do.

Allow God to direct you to those He wants to direct you to for each season. Often it's the little seeds along the way. Many times people have hugged me and prayed with me even when I didn't know how to express how I felt inside and "I don't know" or "it doesn't matter" was about all I could bring myself to say. It mattered that those people gave their time and energy for my healing. I am proud to say that I stand healed today because of Jesus Christ, who was ministered into my life time and time again by good and loving people. Even though many of those people will not see the fruit of their care, or what Jesus has done in me to transform and restore me, my changed life will be a testament to that.

God has sent His people to heal the brokenhearted and to set the captives free. This means God will equip the right people at the right time to support you in being set free, so that in the future you can be the one to help others know Godly freedom. I always had a deep relationship with God, and it is and was God who healed me and it is and was God who will heal you, but companionship and accountability are important on a journey like this. It is very freeing to share your story with others, especially if there are parts of your story or your experiences that you have never been able to share with anyone before. We are not designed by God to keep secrets and hold everything ourselves. More freedom comes through sharing with others. Your pain and sin are not supposed to be kept in darkness. Freedom comes from bringing the light into the darkness. When we tell God and tell another the struggles we carry in our hearts, they begin to be like a burden off our mind.

When we share with another and with God the things we have done wrong and that we are ashamed of, a divine thing happens. A darkened room stops being dark the moment a candle is lit, and the more light we bring into the room the less darkness there is. This is the same for our situations. The light is Jesus, and the truth is light. If something stays hidden and in secret, it remains locked away isolating us from each other, and from God through shame. Sometimes all that is needed is to be able to simply say out loud what we are ashamed of and not have the person react with shock or horror. Then the shame is gone because light has been brought into that situation, and there is no need to be ashamed, and nothing is hidden.

satan wants to divide us and bring disunity because we were not made to be alone and without each other we are weak. We are stronger together than on our own. We are all part of the one body of Christ, and each of us is needed to make up the body. If you don't know who Jesus is bringing you to support you, or if you don't know who you can turn to for support or don't have anyone to talk to about these things, ask God to direct you to the right person. He will provide for you everything you need.

I pray that you will find somebody to support you and share your journey with you. I pray that Jesus in His love will provide somebody to care for you, and stand with you at the right time when you need it. I pray that you will know the support of another on

Choose Life

your journey.

A HOPE THAT GOES BEYOND THIS BOOK

Stand assured that God is bigger than satan. You have no need to be afraid of satan because God is in you. You have more power in the tip of your finger than in all the powers and forces of hell. God in His love restores you. God is so powerful and He can overcome anything for you and in you. Hold steadfast and rest assured in Him. Pray to Him and allow Him on your journey with you. Let Him guide you and take you where you need to go to be able to experience freedom and wholeness.

Don't go looking for the quick fix. Look for the God who restores even if it's a long hard journey. Don't become angry or disheartened if this book did not mean anything to you. That's okay. This book is not meant to help you. This book cannot fix you. It is designed to show you a little of Jesus who restores. Jesus is truth, not this book, and in the time that is right for you He will show you the next stage on your journey with Him. I just shared with you some of my journey and a few things I learnt along the way in the hope that it might help you find God and, through Him, find who you are and your freedom from your pains and a joy that goes deep into your soul.

In the hard times know there is a hope, a hope for you that goes far beyond this book. You are secure and set free in Christ Jesus. I am not saying it will be easy, but know His promise for you, not just for eternity in Heaven but for your beautiful life of freedom now. Don't give up and don't give in because Jesus stands shoulder to shoulder with you with a mighty power and a deep compassion. Let Him wrap His arms around you, fall into Him and let Him hold you. Walk with Jesus and continue to pray and read your Bible. Through doing that you turn towards the light. Do not turn to the darkness. Keep firm to the light and hold fast to the loving Lord Jesus Christ who is full of such grace and healing.

What is important now is that you look to Jesus and ask Him to fill you and shape you. He is the One who will hold you steady and keep you secure in His loving arms. Fall into Him and allow Him to do His work in you.

It is my prayer now for you that God meets you here today and that you will be filled more and more with

Holy Spirit and that as you walk with Him you are able to hear Him as He guides you. I pray provision for your needs and healing for your soul, body, and Spirit. I pray that the hope you have in Him becomes a very real hope for you, and I pray that you find freedom now and continue to find freedom all the days of your life. I pray that Jesus shapes and moulds you to His way. I thank Him that the old has gone and the new has come, and I pray that God meets you in your healing need. Amen.

ABOUT THE AUTHOR

From Manchester UK, Joanna grew up in a loving Christian home, however Joanna was bullied in her early years at school and faced other difficulties. Through it she grew to have a low opinion of herself, and a distorted idea of who she was. Yet she had a profound relationship with God from a young age. It was through the love, care, and ministry of Jesus into her life through those who met Joanna in the wilderness she had found herself in, that Joanna was able to see that freedom from her pain, and deep inner joy and peace were possible.

Joanna's own experience as a hurting teenager and young woman was that the church didn't always know how to help her; they had no answer for the pain. So she felt lost inside the church, and they weren't always able to support her.

Joanna recommitted her life to serve Jesus when she was 16-years-old visiting a village in east Africa. But it was 12 years later before she was able to walk in freedom.

In her pain, Joanna had made bad choices, through

which she hurt those in the church who had set out to help her. This lead to her feeling a huge sense of guilt, shame and condemnation, as well as rejection, abandonment and fear. This lead Joanna to come to the end of herself, and her trust in God and His church, which forced her to make a choice; life or death. She chose life and so set out to seek help and support. That was 6 years after she first visited that African village.

It has been another 6 years on the journey, with many new people from God's church coming alongside her. Joanna is now healed, restored and redeemed in Jesus, excited for the new path He will take her on.

She is currently studying a degree in Theology, Mission and Evangelism with Chester University. She is passionate to see the church of Christ set free and made whole in God and through God. She believes that those who are broken and hurting in the church need just as much love, compassion and understanding as those outside of the church. She is passionate about sharing the tools to freedom she has learnt along her way. Joanna's prayer for God's church is to see it whole and restored in Him.

In Chester and beyond, Joanna is involved in reaching the hurting, lost and broken with the message of freedom and love in Christ. Joanna recognizes the lost and the broken are in our churches every Sunday morning, as well as being out there in the rough of the streets. Joanna believes the bride (the church) can be as beautiful as the bridegroom (Jesus).

Joanna is passionate about seeing healing and wholeness in Christ where there is brokenness. Joanna is passionate about sharing freedom and the love of Christ with others.

If you would like to get in touch with Joanna for any reason, she would love to hear from you, or if you are looking for information on where you can find more support in your pain, or with your faith walk towards healing, you can do so by visiting the website below:

www.joannadouglas.wix.com/truefreedombooks

May the Lord Jesus Christ bless you, now and forever more. Amen.

TRUTH OF CHRIST STATEMENTS

- I have been healed. (Isaiah 53:5)

- I am a new creation. (2 Corinthians 5:17)

- I am clean. (John 15:3)

- I am more than a conqueror through Christ, who loves me.(Romans 8:37)

- I have been made righteous. (2 Corinthians 5:21)

- I am a child of God and one in Christ. (Galatians 3:26, 28)

- I am being changed into the likeness of Christ. (2 Corinthians 3:18)

- I am like Christ. (1 John 4:10)

- I have life. (1 John 5:12)

- I am chosen and appointed by Christ to bear His fruit. (John 15:16)

- I am Christ's friend. (John 15:15)

- Christ Himself is in me. (Colossians 1:27)

- I am blameless and free from accusation. (Colossians 1:22)

- I am a member of a chosen race, a royal priesthood, a holy nation, a People for God's own possession. (1 Peter 2:9,10)

- I am born of God, and satan cannot touch me. (1 John 5:8)

- I am a child of God and I will resemble Christ when He returns. (1 John 3:1,2)

- I am loved. (1 John 4:10)

- I have been sealed with the Holy Spirit. (Ephesians 1:13)

- I have been raised up and seated with Christ in Heaven. (Ephesians 2:6)

- I am more than a conqueror through Christ, who loves me. (Romans 8:37)

- I have been given peace. (John 14:27)

www.ingramcontent.com/pod-product-compliance
Lightning Source LLC
Chambersburg PA
CBHW022112040426
42450CB00006B/665